5 - 13 -79

Mom,

hope you can use and
enjoy this book. You're
a great mother and I
hope you have a great
day .

Lots of love,

your son Rick

# The Pocket
# Wine Book

# THE POCKET WINE BOOK

## An Authoritative Consumer Guide

### BOB EVANS &
### ROBERT WILKINSON

The Apotheca Press, Ltd.

International Standard Book Number:
   0-930002-00-8
Library of Congress Catalog Card Number:
   77-86014
The Apotheca Press, Ltd., Atlanta, Georgia
© 1978 by The Apotheca Press, Ltd
All Rights Reserved
Printed in the United States of America
Designed by Robert Wilkinson

TO JOHN AND JEAN PAYNE
FOR WHOM THIS BOOK WAS WRITTEN

# CONTENTS

# ACKNOWLEDGMENTS

TO give credit to everyone who has helped in the research and production of this book would require an enormous effort of the memory. Let us simply express our deepest appreciation to the following for their assistance and consideration, their concern and encouragement—they have all, in various ways, made this enterprise possible:

Mr. John Avery & Averys of Bristol Ltd.; Dr. Fred Beech; Mr. Michael Berrendt; Hr. Winfried Berres & Weingut Wwe. Hugo Berres; Bischöfliches Weingüter, Trier; M. & Mme. André Brunet; Mr. & Mrs. Ed & Doris Buckner; the University Library, Cambridge; Mr. Richard Carothers; M. Philippe Castéja & Borie-Manoux, Bordeaux; M. Jean-Louis Chave; M. Michel Cornier & the French Trade Commission; M. Paul Coulon & Domaine de Beaurenard; M. Delbecq & Ch. Ausone; the board of directors of Down the Hatch, Atlanta, Ga.; M. Philippe Dubos; Mr. Doug Eason & Rose Printing Co.; Ms. Pam Evans; Mr. & Mrs. Bill & Buttercup Garrad; Mr. & Mrs. John & Amy Harris; Dr. Hermann & Weingut J.J. Christoffel-Erben; Hr. Engelbert Hillen; Mr. Peter Hoffman; Mr. Timothy Johnston; Hr. Albert Kallfelz; Hôtel Lameloise, Chagny; M. Hubert Lamy; Mr. Louis Langdon; Fr. Annie Lay; Mr. Melvyn Master; Hr. & Fr. Hans Mechow & Hotel zur Post, Ürzig; Hr. Egon Müller; Dr. Richard & Frl. Barbara Müller & Rudolf Müller, K.G.; Mr. Beau Newton; Mr. Peter Norris; Mr. & Mrs. John & Jean Payne; the late Mr. Noel Priestley; M. Roland Rapet; Hr. Max Ferdinand & Dr. Dirk Richter; Schloss Johannisberg; Schloss Vollrads; Mr. Victor Schwieger; Staatliches Weinbaudomänen, Trier; Staatsweingüter, Kloster Eberbach; Mr. Dante Stephensen; Mr. Warren B. Strauss; Mr. Christopher Tatham; Frl. Thanisch & Weingut Wwe. Dr. H. Thanisch; M. Léon Thienpont & Vieux Ch. Certan; M. Tisserand & Domaine Fleurot-Larose; M. Roger Tissier & L'Éventail de Vignerons Producteurs, Corcelles-en-Beaujolais; Ms. Elaine Tramell; Dr. William Tuthill; Ms. Rita Wilkinson; Winzergenossenschaft Erbach; Mr. James Woolard; Hr. Wolfgang Zahn; M. Jacques Zurfluh.

# PREFACE

THERE is almost a latent sense of evangelism behind the writing of this book. The whole enterprise has been based on the deeply-felt conviction that wine is a glorious and entirely accessible thing that has been shrouded, quite unnecessarily, in a dense fog of mystery. It seemed obvious, from the inception of this project, that few of us are in a position to enjoy the luxury of a casual promenade through the literature of wine in search of explanations that are of little value except to the initiated. *The Pocket Wine Book* is an attempt to reduce wine knowledge to a manageable reality: as such, it is not aimed exclusively at the reader who is already fluent in the detailed grammar of wine. It is above all a *consumer* publication, and sets out with the modest but important goal of simplicity.

*The Pocket Wine Book* is divided into three basic sections. *Part One: A Background* is a technical introduction to vines and vinification: its use is entirely optional except as a source of background information. *Part Two: The Essentials* we feel to be indispensable; its five chapters representing the flesh and bones of consumer survival. The *Reference* section is exactly what its title implies—a comprehensive guide to the wines of Germany and France, indexed in detail for immediate reference.

Throughout this book, we have inevitably drawn on the great fund of knowledge that appears in the professional literature, and we have acknowledged the best of our sources in the *Bibliography*. The *Reference* section, on the other hand, is far from conventional in that it actually provides a rating system for the most important wines of each area, ordered in a series of tables set lengthways on the page. This is possibly the first such publication to take on that major responsibility. Our inclusions and ratings are based on a combination of personal experience, current trade opinion, and general availablity on the American market. We have tried to be as thorough and conscientious as possible, while realizing that a task of this magnitude is likely to lead us into areas of considerable debate. Our general feeling, however, is that the hazards of such a venture are well worth the risk—real consumer knowledge unequivocally requires a positive commitment to opinion.

Although this book was conceived over a glass of port, its *Reference* section is limited to the wines of Germany and France. The reasons are twofold: first, German and French wines are probably the most significant imports—in terms of overall quality—to appear in the United States; secondly, this book is ultimately a reflection of personal experience, and it is in these countries that our knowledge principally lies.

Again, we believe wine to be a comprehensible phenomenon, and we have tried, in every aspect of this book, to be genuinely useful to the non-professional consumer. *The Pocket Wine Book* is presented in its portable format precisely because we want it to be used—a working guide that is perhaps a little uncomfortable on the ubiquitous coffee table. We feel it is an honest book, emerging from a very real love for the beauty and integrity of our subject. If we find that wine has become just a little more meaningful to our readers, then we consider our purpose to be valid.

*Bob Evans*                                   *Robert Wilkinson*

# Part One
# A Background

# One
# The Ecology of Wine

TO follow the path of the Mosel on a bleak winter's day is to feel some basic, elemental power. Vineyard paths, courted by clouds, crawl awkwardly through sleeping vines, which fall like ordered cataracts into the tiny river below. Yet this impossible, dramatically beautiful land of gray cliffs and slate soil, so totally unsuited to the usual ways of man, is among the most valuable property in Germany. Precisely what it is that draws such a spectacular wine from the growth of those hills is the real magic of the vine, an absurdity of nature that would seem to triumph where all else might fail. In this chapter, we will look at the place of the vine in the natural world, and consider those factors that are necessary to its success.

4

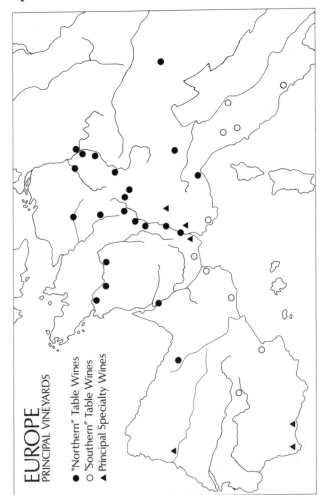

EUROPE
PRINCIPAL VINEYARDS

● "Northern" Table Wines
○ "Southern" Table Wines
▲ Principal Specialty Wines

### THE VINE

Of the many species of vine that have grown wild since prehistory, there is only one, known botanically as *Vitis vinifera*, that is fundamentally responsible for the production of quality wine. Originating in southern Russia, *Vitis vinifera* was slowly carried, through migration and trade, to the Greek settlements of the Mediterranean, and onwards to Rome. From here, the expansion of the Roman Empire established viticulture across the continent of Europe and thus formed the locational basis of modern vineyards. Yet, despite the forces of politics and history, responsibility for the success of the vine must remain the ultimate and special province of nature.

### CLIMATE

Apart from the intervention of man, it is climate—and more specifically temperature—that is the single most important factor in determining the growth of vines. *Vitis vinifera* is a sensitive and demanding plant, requiring not only the full benefits of summer heat, but also a moderation in winter conditions to ensure its survival. Its distribution in the northern hemisphere, therefore, is defined quite logically by the limits of a climatic zone that covers most of western Europe as far north as Mainz and Paris, and parts of the United States down into Mexico. Within that zone, there are certain limited areas where, by virtue of the nature of local microclimates, *Vitis vinifera* will simply not survive.

The most critical time for the vintner is, of course, the growing season, which will begin with the budding of the vine in spring and continue until autumn harvest *(vintage)*. Within the Mediterranean countries, it is generally true that summer temperatures are excessive. Hot growing seasons will saturate the grape with natural sugar, producing wines that are high in alcohol. Acidity is reduced, and the wines lose the ability to establish a satisfactory acid balance, which is critical to the production of good table wine. It is roughly true to say that the only quality wines to emerge from Mediterranean regions are either the result of the intervention of the vintner (the fortified wines of Spain and Portugal), or brought about by the benevolent micro-climates of exceptional areas (in France, the southern Rhône; along with many parts of Italy, and the Spanish Rioja). Otherwise, the table wines of southern Europe are generally characterized as rough and alcoholic.

Moving northwards, we come to the areas that are exclusively responsible for the finest table wines in the world. The climate changes dramatically. Winters are cold, springs unpredictable, and the summers vary enormously in temperature and rainfall. The days are a little shorter here, and the location of vineyards with regard to the sun takes on a special importance. Since the grapes will often be lower in natural sugar, their alcohol potential is proportionately reduced. The total acidity of the grape increases, along with a change in its internal balance. Since climatic conditions are less brutal, the steady growth of the vine can now produce the subtlest of fruits. The real charm of the wines of Germany, for instance, is largely attributable to a peculiar equilibrium of sugar and acid, which can only be accomplished in the temperate lands of the north. Micro-climates are clearly critical here. In Bordeaux, for instance, where the vines are already in bud in April, the dangers of a late spring frost are enormous: not only are the young shoots killed, so reducing the crop for that year, but the yield of further years is crippled until new branches can form.

## THE SOIL

The role of the soil in determining the quality of the vine has been much exaggerated. Certainly it contains vital nutrients whose resources are finite, and vines must be planted at strategic intervals to maximize absorption (preferably in the absence of other crops, unlike the primitive holdings of certain parts of S. Europe). Like any other plant, vines also require moisture, and limited rainfall must necessarily be retained in the ground for as long as it is useful. Of paramount importance, however, is the ability of the soil to drain water, and the reasons are essentially indirect. Under good drainage conditions, the soil becomes significantly more capable of heat retention, a factor that is critical in climates where evening temperatures are otherwise cool. Hence the universal tendency of good vines to thrive on sloping, stony ground, often draining the water through layers of chalk and holding the day's heat in surface stones.

The success of the vine, therefore, is predetermined by sun and soil, and the myriad other whims of the natural cycle. Yet wine, itself, as the fermented juice of grapes, is the province of man, its production subject to all his works and inventions, his genius—and, alas, his foolishness. The remarkable and complex process of vinification is discussed in Chapter Two.

# Two
# How Wine is Made

TO cross the vineyard road, from one tasting to another, is not to be bored by repetition. It is an altogether familiar experience that two wines, from precisely the same region of origin, can taste entirely different when they are the products of separate vintners. Although the principles of wine making are really quite simple, the art (and science) of wine goes well beyond the whims of climate, the selection of grapes, and geographical origin. Making wine is easy, but to make wine well requires an exceptional combination of skills, and an abundance of that rare commodity known only as integrity. It is that singular ability of the good wine maker to understand and direct the many subtleties of vinification that places him—and his wines—apart.

We are concerned in this chapter with the general scope of the wine making process.

THE GRAPE

By the time the pickers' carts roll down the
vineyard road at harvest, the grape has reached its
critical state of succulent ripeness. Some three quar-
ters of its fleshy pulp are water, which will com-
prise the bulk of the *must*—the unfermented
crushed fruit from which the wine will be made.
The remaining parts are mostly sugar, along with
small quantities of other carbohydrates, acids,
vitamins, and traces of various other substances, including enzymes and minerals. We are concerned
here with those components that will be of fundamental importance in the vinification process:

*Sugars*
In *Vitis vinifera* there are two primary sugars, dex-
trose and levulose (known also as glucose and fructose), which occur in roughly equal proportions.
Their quantities will vary with the climatic
qualities of the vintage, and the ripeness of the
grape at harvest.

*Acids*
Tartaric and malic are the principal grape acids,
normally accompanied by citric acid in significantly smaller quantities. It is tartaric acid that remains distinct in the wine after the vinification
process is complete, retaining many of the original
qualities of the fresh grape. The fate of malic acid is
discussed later in this chapter in the section on
malo-lactic fermentation. The original acidity of the
grape will be of particular importance, not only in

contributing major elements of taste, but also as a factor in the promotion of the wine's biological stability.

*Tannins*
Although tannins occur naturally in the skins, stems, and seeds, it is the skins that are their primary source within the grape, since the stems are normally removed before fermentation, and the seeds are preserved intact so as to prevent the release into the must of certain undesirable chemicals. Tannins are complex acidic substances that contribute significantly to the longevity, flavor, and color of the wine. (Also present in the skins are pigments, similarly complex, known as *anthocyanins*, which react with tannins to determine the final color of wines produced by on-skin fermentation.)

FERMENTATION

Towards the end of the growing season, millions of micro-organisms called *yeasts* settle on the outer surface of the skins of ripe grapes, eventually apparent in a fine, dull bloom. It is the action of yeasts, or rather the enzymes they contain that is the very basis of the fermentation process. In 1810, the great French chemist, Gay-Lussac, reduced the principles of fermentation to a simple chemical equation, whereby sugar is converted, through the action of yeast enzymes (called *ferments*), into ethyl alcohol and carbon dioxide. Present in different areas in different combinations, individual strains of wild yeasts impart their own special characteristics that are contributing factors to the distinctive qualities of a particular wine. Today, local yeasts are frequently isolated under laboratory conditions to produce pure and predictable cultures that offer the cautious vintner an important element of control. Fermentation is, of course, an entirely natural phenomenon, only monitored and adjusted by the wine maker to free it as far as possible from any secondary reaction that might endanger the quality of the product.

Once the grapes have been picked, they are quickly stemmed and crushed, then transferred immediately to the fermenting vat so that fermentation, which begins shortly after the skins are broken and the sugar exposed, can occur under conditions of maximum control. The process itself is quite dramatic and usually short-lived, an impressive activity of much heaving and bubbling that, in the case of the majority of wines, is complete within a week. Left to its own devices, the must will continue to ferment until some 14% of its volume has been converted into alcohol (at which point yeasts become chemically inactive) or until the entirety of its sugar has been consumed.

The wine maker is now faced with his first major decision as to the "style" of the wine he wishes to produce. If his grapes were low in natural sugar, he may choose to stop fermentation unnaturally through the addition of sulfur dioxide, leaving a degree of residual sugar proportionate to the desired level of sweetness of the final product. This is particularly true of many of the low-alcohol sweet wines of Germany. Under different conditions, fermentation might proceed to completion to create a wine that is dry on the palate, but high in alcohol—as is the case in Burgundy. In practice, of course, the nature of the vintage, and the requirements of local and house traditions will normally reduce the decision to a matter of simple intuition.

Temperature control is critical throughout fermentation. While yeast cells function adequately over a broad temperature range (anywhere from 50°F. to 90°F., although narrower parameters are preferable), their effectiveness is doubtful when temperatures go beyond the usual limits. Since autumn days can be far from cool, and fermentation itself produces much additional heat, precautions must be taken to keep cellar conditions at least within the range of acceptability to avert deactivation of the yeasts, apart from inviting the intervention of harmful bacteria. Whatever the circumstances, the process must be chemically complete before the vintner can even begin to make adequate wine.

### RED WINES

Grape juice is universally pale in color: to a great extent, red wines are red and white wines white simply as the result of the presence or absence of skins during fermentation. For red wines, therefore, the grapes, complete with skins and pips (now shapeless after stemming and crushing) are pumped into vats for fermentation. The skins and pulp gradually rise above the fermenting juice to form a dense *chapeau,* or *hat,* at the top of the vat, an otherwise separate layer that must be constantly reintegrated with the underlying juice. As we have already seen, the skins of grapes (and also their pips) contain tannins which, amongst other things, prolong both the maturation and life span of the wine. A decision, therefore, as to how long the wine will be *vatted,* or allowed to sit on the skins and pulp after fermentation has died down, comes back again to the central issue of style. It is frequently claimed that the public has forced the industry to make its wines to be consumed young. It is perhaps less easy to determine the nature of public sentiment than it is to see the economic advantages of keeping inventories in a state of constant turnover. The great days when a big red Burgundy or a middle-class claret were vatted for many weeks are now perpetuated only by those few exceptional estates who can still afford to rate the virtues of quality higher than the mechanics of profit.

When the wine has been satisfactorily fermented, it is run off into oak barrels for aging (*free-run wine*) and the remaining pulp is pressed and piped into separate barrels for blending, or to be sold in the local market (*press wine*). At this point, the wine is still quite cloudy and must undergo several stages of natural and induced clarification. Left to rest, it produces a thick early deposit called *lees,* which is separated or *racked* from the free liquid by pumping the latter into fresh barrels. In the meantime, the wine is absorbing oxygen from the atmosphere through the wood, and is simultaneously evaporating back out. To reduce the risk of bacterial spoilage, the barrels are frequently topped to reduce any air space, or *ullage*.

As the wine approaches readiness for bottling, it undergoes a final stage of induced clarification, which can be achieved in several different ways. Traditionally, it is *fined*: egg white, blood, or other clotting agents are added at the top of the barrel and gradually sink to the bottom, taking with them any remaining substances suspended in the wine. Today, fining has been supplemented by filtration and the centrifuge, which, in increasing cases of total replacement, have become significant factors in the production of bulk wine of mediocre quality.

The first six to nine months of barrel age are more or less mandatory if only to bring the wine to a state of chemical stability for safe bottling. After that, it is a question of the attitude of the vintner (and the properties of his product) as to the quality of the wine he wishes to produce. Beaujolais, which prides itself on the youthful freshness of many of its wines, will often bottle only a matter of months after vintage, while in Bordeaux the greater growths will frequently have undergone as much as two years of barrel age, an absolute necessity for expensive wines of established character. It is thus the "luxury" years that will see gradual, more complex changes; the wine becoming a deeper, less brilliant red, exhibiting new, subtler tastes of softness and depth. As the wine soaks slowly into the wood, the wood, in return, gives the wine tannin and flavor. Finally a bouquet emerges. After the last stages of racking and clarification, the wine may now be blended: either from within the vintage to equalize the special qualities of individual casks; or with other wines to create products of less specific origin. The wine is now ready for bottling.

## WHITE WINES

The vinification of white wine is distinct from the very beginning. The grapes are crushed and pressed immediately after harvest, thereby separating both skins and stalks so that the pale juice can be left to ferment alone. Furthermore, while red wines are predominantly dry, whites are frequently sweet and can be made that way in a number of fashions. In theory of course, the classic sweet whites contain a sufficiently high percentage of natural sugar in the grape that some is left over after fermentation is complete. Yet, as we have already discussed, in instances where nature has been less generous—and also in frequent practice to provide predictability— fermentation is stopped by the inhibitory action of sulfur dioxide. Sugar may also be added to the must (*chaptalization* is considered later in this chapter), but the practice is delicate and frequently abused.

Since color extraction is not necessary, white wines are fermented at generally lower temperatures than reds and under slower, more controlled conditions. As a result, the wines are potentially higher in alcohol and retain substantially more of the fresh original qualities of the fruit— hence the exquisite delicacy of, for example, a great white Burgundy or an early-picked Mosel. In some areas, the grapes are even fermented under pressure in order to maximize control of rate and temperature, although fermentation is more commonly slowed down by the use of frequent rackings. After fermentation, aging proceeds much as with reds, but again often at lower temperatures. Since the current market seems particularly concerned with the absolute clarity of the product (and the reasons are entirely cosmetic), cool cellar conditions are significant in allowing for the precipitation of any remaining cloudiness before reaching the consumer. After several finings and rackings, the wine reaches a point of stability, is aged according to the usual factors of regional custom, the inherent properties of the wine, and the simple economics of storage— and is then ready to be bottled.

### ROSÉS

Little need be said about rosés, except that they are, hopefully, not the work of an alchemist, nor the result of a carefree blending of red and white. For the most part, rosés are made from red grapes whose skins are left in the fermenting vat just long enough to produce their characteristic pigmentation. Although rosés often make for pleasant drinking, they are never great wines, and attitudes toward their vinification vary accordingly.

## MALO-LACTIC FERMENTATION

Under most cellar conditions, a secondary fermentation will tend to occur naturally in wines of certain acid strengths, unless deliberate measures are taken to prevent it. Known as malo-lactic fermentation, it is quite distinct from primary fermentation in that it is not concerned with the conversion of sugar into alcohol: rather, it is the result of the actions of certain bacteria in converting malic acid into lactic acid and carbon dioxide (along with small quantities of pyruvic acid). It is malic acid that is to a great extent responsible for the sharp qualities of unripe grapes, and is frequently present in significant proportions at vintage. Lactic acid, on the other hand, is a softer, more palatable substance, and represents a desirable change from the high-acid wines of certain areas (Switzerland is a major example). Apart from a reduction in apparent acidity (and other means are available), the process also produces certain by-products that can subtly enhance the complexity and flavor of the product.

The principal advantage of malo-lactic fermentation, however, is the stabilization of the wine against further attack by bacteria. If conditions are right for the action of one set of bacteria, they are also right for the action of others. Bad strains can ruin a wine and must therefore be subject to identification and control: if the process is to occur, it must be completed satisfactorily before bottling, while the bacteria are still accessible to detection. Furthermore, malo-lactic fermentation itself, if incomplete, will produce distinct, often unpleasant odors and even cloudiness (apart from unwanted carbon dioxide*) which will be trapped irretrievably within the bottle.

Thus, in the absence of other means of deacidification and bacteriological control, the reaction must be carefully monitored—even induced, then stopped if bottling is to occur early since, under normal cellar conditions, it may not begin until many months after vintage.

### SPARKLING WINE

There are a number of ways of making wine sparkle, ranging from infusion with carbon dioxide in the fashion of soda pop (the results are particularly poor), to the complexities of the lengthy process that will eventually produce Champagne. A wine will effervesce quite naturally if fermentation of any sort is allowed to continue in the bottle: although this simple discovery probably represents the genesis of sparkling wine, its practice without refinement is now limited to inexpensive wines destined only for local markets. We are concerned here with the two methods that are of primary importance in the present-day trade.

---

*Notable exceptions are the sparkling wines of the Minho district of northern Portugal, and certain wines from Italy. Here, in-bottle malo-lactic fermentation is a deliberate part of the wine making process. Their quality is never exceptional.

*Champagne*

The *Champagne method*, or *méthode champenoise*, is based on an induced secondary fermentation in the bottle, converting added sugar into alcohol and carbon dioxide. A study in expense, care, and prolonged hard work, it alone is responsible for sparkling wines of exceptional quality. Although originating in the Champagne region of France, where it had reached a level of industrial standardization by the 1830's, its principles have been applied to the premium sparkling wine industry throughout the world. The process begins with a lengthy primary fermentation to produce a medium-acid wine of approximately 11% alcoholic strength. The wine is racked in the usual fashion then blended with wines from other vineyards (and frequently other vintages) to produce what is known in Champagne as a *cuvée*, a distinctive blend that is representative of the traditional style of the shipper. After six months or so of further aging and clarification, the very special practices of Champagne making become particularly apparent. Cane sugar is added to separate casks of aged wine to produce a sweet syrup, known as *liqueur de tirage*. Together with appropriate strains of cultured yeast, the syrup is now used to innoculate the *cuvée* in final readiness for bottling. Thus a slow, induced fermentation commences in the bottle and proceeds in cool cellars for a period of several months. The bottles, tightly capped to accommodate the gradual build-up of internal pressure, are stacked horizontally, beginning a long process of steady aging that will often continue for three, four, or even five years.

The sediment produced by secondary fermentation causes a fine cloud within the wine which, to this day, is removed by the traditional method of *remuage*. It is the daily job of the *remueur* to gradually bring each bottle to a vertical position, cork down, through the use of a special frame: as he moves the bottle he shakes it, thereby freeing the sediment to settle in the neck of the eventually inverted bottle. The neck is chilled and the cork removed, the pressure ejecting a mixture of wine and sediment in the form of a neatly frozen "plug" (*dégorgement*).

Before the bottle is corked for the last time, a second syrup is prepared and added in accordance with the desired style of the product. Known as *liqueur d'éxpédition*, it is made from aged wine, cane sugar, and small quantities of high quality brandy for stabilization: the size of the dose will be directly responsible for the wine's eventual label—that often unnoticed sweetness factor, ranging from *Brut* at one extreme to Sweet, or *Doux*, at the other. At last, the wine is allowed to rest, the final aging slumber before the eventual moment of sale. A period of as much as seven years may have elapsed since vintage, seven years of corking and recorking, twisting and shaking, fermenting and sweetening, all for the sake of that fizzy, golden delight we know only as Champagne.

*Charmat*
The *Charmat*, or *tank method*, was developed in

France in 1910 by one Eugène Charmat, and is now used extensively in the large-scale production of sparkling wines of good, but rarely spectacular quality. The tank method is the commercial realization of the Champagne principle on an industrial scale, the *cuvée* fermented not in the bottle, but rather in large pressurized tanks. Each tank (Charmat's original concept required four) contributes its own essential factor in the process, ranging from rapid maturation through temperature change, to yeasting, sugaring and clarification. The fundamental disadvantage of the tank system is the absence of prolonged yeast contact, in comparison with the Champagne method, which requires years of slow reaction with the lees. It is precisely this gradual aging of the wine on its own sediment that imparts to Champagne those special subtleties of flavor and bouquet.

### FORTIFIED WINES

*Fortification* is the addition of brandy to a wine at some point in its vinification, resulting in an alcohol content of some 18% to 20%. The practice, which began with the British shipping trade in the eighteenth century, is principally confined to the Iberian Peninsula (notably port, sherry, and Madeira), although fortified wines are produced elsewhere in Europe, but rarely appear on the American market.

*Port*

Taking its name from the Portuguese town of Oporto, from which it is traditionally shipped, port is made by the addition of brandy to halt fermentation. The alcohol level is proportionately raised, leaving the wine with a characteristic degree of natural sugar. After aging and blending with other casks, the younger wines are sold as *ruby port*, while those whose pigmentation has browned with further age enter the market as the more expensive *tawny ports*. *Vintage port* is entirely distinct in that the greater part of its maturation occurs in the bottle, not the wood. Since vintages are declared by the Oporto shippers only in exceptional years, vintage port is normally outstanding in both quality and price. (It is not to be confused with *late-bottled port*, which is wine of a particular vintage that has undergone prolonged barrel age, for bottling at a later date.) For a discussion of the problems associated with port sediment *(crust)*, see Chapter Four.

*Sherry*

Originating in the Jerez district of southern Spain, sherry differs from port at the very beginning. The entirety of its sugar is fermented to produce a wine that is initially completely dry—at first in the absence of air, and subsequently, for a period of several months, in open barrels. Peculiar to sherry country (and also to the French Jura) is the natural growth of a thick, yeasty film on the surface of the wine, called *flor*. Throughout the first year of vinification, each barrel is carefully monitored for its tendency (through the complex variables of microbiology) to produce this remarkable growth. Those that do are given a moderate dose of brandy and become *finos*, while those that do not are more heavily dosed and later sold as *olorosos*. A further peculiarity of sherry is its aging process, which works through the action of a *solera*, a long series of interdependent barrels containing wine in a state of constant blend. As sherry is drawn off at one end, it is refilled at the other with wine of a similar character, thus perpetuating the quality of a system that might easily have been begun at the turn of the century. *Finos* can occur as *manzanillas* (the dryest of all, with those peculiar tastes of their coastal aging), or in their aged form as (true) *amontillados*. *Olorosos* tend to be heavier in body, reaching the extremes of richness in the sweetened *cream sherries* that were developed by the merchants of Bristol. (Some of the latter have, alas, suffered in quality in recent years as the result of enormous popular demand.)

*Madeira*
The Portuguese island of Madeira, located some 500 miles from Lisbon, has given its name to fortified wines of particular longevity. The wine is fully fermented, then lightly fortified, after which it is actually heated (*baked*) for a period of several months at temperatures of approximately 110°F. (although the reasons for this exceptional practice are partly historical, it does, in fact, bring about a rapid and beneficial aging). A further fortification precedes a final blending, which will determine the various grades of sweetness associated with the grapes of

origin, ranging from *Sercial* (the dryest) to *Bual* (considerably sweeter), and *Malmsey* (or *Malvasia*, the richest of all).

### BOTTLE AGE

A wine, once bottled, will continue to undergo significant chemical change but, as with any organic material, the factors that control the complex and frequently unpredictable process we call aging are only partly understood.

Pasteur pointed out in the 1860s that aging presupposes the presence of oxygen, although in strictly limited quantities. While sitting in the barrel, the wine is slowly absorbing small quantities of oxygen through the wood, and much greater quantities during bottling itself: but Pasteur's original contention that there is a constant, but minute flow of air through the cork has now been shown to be essentially incorrect. The wine bottle is a sealed environment; its contents dependent for their critical supply of oxygen entirely upon the air space in the neck of the bottle, and the oxygen already dissolved in the wine itself. Thus the ratio of air space to volume of wine is important in the relative aging of various bottle sizes: a half-bottle, for example, will age significantly quicker than a magnum (which has four times the volume of wine, but only slightly more air).

Interestingly enough, in red wines the change in coloring matter is of fundamental importance to the aging process. Color is constituted entirely by the

combined properties of tannins and anthocyanins
(Chapter Two, p. 11): these are oxidized to form a
sediment, the color changing from a deep, often
brilliant, purplish red to an aged, almost orange
brown. Independently, alcohols and acids react to
form esters, while aldehydes are produced through
the oxidation of alcohol. Both esters and aldehydes
are volatile and of primary importance in the formation of a wine's bouquet. As tannins continue to
be lost in the form of sediment (now joining with
aldehydes and precipitating with proteins), so
much of the obvious astringency and acidity of
youth diminishes.

In white wines, however, it is frequently the very
freshness and acidity of the fruit that makes them
special, qualities of flavor and aroma that will fade
with age. Furthermore, since their tannin content
tends to be considerably lower, they are often far
more pleasant to drink young than might be a red
wine of similar quality. On the other hand, the
greater whites mature impressively with prolonged
bottle age, their color changing gradually to the
deepest of yellows, even golden brown in the case
of old Sauternes, wines which have absorbed large
amounts of tannin from years of sitting in the
wood. (Tannins in isolation are actually yellow,
changing to brown when oxidized.)

In general, therefore, the aging of wine is
basically dependent on the oxidation and support
reactions of its various compounds, beginning in the
barrel and continuing under sealed conditions in
the bottle. Ultimately, it is the gradual blending and
apparent softening of the many components that

make up a young wine that will produce a coherent, palatable taste. The time factors involved will vary enormously from wine to wine and from vintage to vintage: a great claret, for example, may require decades before it reaches its peak, while a Beaujolais *nouveau* may have died within six months of bottling. Essentially, it is a question of what was in the grapes to begin with, and the course of vinification that followed: the peculiarities of the vintage, and that recurring, central issue of style.

## ADDITIONAL METHODS

There are really two purposes to the vintner's additional intervention in the natural wine making process: he is concerned with producing as good and characteristic a product as he can from the varying qualities of his grapes, and he is also preoccupied with the issue of biological and chemical stability. The following refinements are of basic importance:

*Sulfuring*
Used extensively throughout the wine producing areas of the world, the addition of sulfur dioxide (usually in solution as sulfurous acid) is of key importance throughout the vinification process. Its contribution to wine making has been well known since the Middle Ages. It is important as an antiseptic (both of wines and containers) and as an agent in the control of harmful bacteria. It is an antioxidant, and is instrumental in the retardation or suppression of fermentation. It is also a clarifying agent,

and aids in the preservation of color. Excessive sulfur is of obvious odor, and must therefore be carefully controlled before bottling.

*Pasteurization*
Normally performed in flash bulk, or by a rapid heating and cooling of the bottle, as a means of destroying harmful bacteria and giving the wine chemical and physical stability. Since it renders the wine inert, it is not capable of further subleties of aging, and is therefore of no value whatsoever in the production of anything other than wines of less than the best quality for mass consumption.

*Chaptalization*
The addition of cane sugar (sucrose) to the must before fermentation. The sucrose is converted naturally to natural grape sugars, and fermentation proceeds in the usual fashion. As a means of raising the eventual alcohol content of the wine, it can be used to advantage, but is subject to frequent abuse. Practiced widely in Burgundy and in the Q.b.A. classes of German wines. Named after its creator, Dr. Jean Chaptal (1756-1832).

*Süssreserve*
A clever German technique, whereby unfermented or partially fermented grape juice is separated from the bulk of the must. Once the wine is stable after a full fermentation, the *Süssreserve* is added just prior to bottling, and the product is thereby sweetened. Now practiced widely in Germany, it is a sensible way of producing wines of consistent stability and

palatable sweetness in the absence of adequate grapes. Its flavor, however, is quite distinct to the trained palate and is frowned upon by purists.

*Acidification*
The addition of tartaric (or, occasionally, citric) acid to grapes deficient in natural acidity after long hot summers. Normally added to the must before fermentation for maximum blending effect.

# Part Two
# The Essentials

# Three
# The Business of Wine

THE functioning of the American wine trade is probably the least understood and most under-emphasized facet of the consumer's comprehension of this thing we call wine. It is as much a key to value as is knowing how the wine was made, its vintage and producer, and the region it came from. In all cases, wine is made to be sold: the trade is the commercial functioning of a specialized agricultural and industrial process. Since many of the products we see on the retailers' shelves have been designed with the express purpose of making particularly high profits, we have to consider the ways in which wine is treated and marketed in order to grasp and identify the genuine stuff of the vintner's art.

An important wine maker from the Mosel was recently asked at a tasting in Florida why his Ockfener Bockstein was more expensive than that of another producer, whereupon he quoted the old Mosel proverb that Ockfener Bockstein can also be made from grapes! As long as wine is a commercial enterprise there will be those who wish to capitalize on the success of genuine products by fooling the consumer into a false belief that what he can offer at half the price is just as good. There are many instances of genuine values in wine, but many also of poor products. There are a lot of grapes in this world and somehow they all seem to go somewhere. Furthermore, the massive increase in the popularity of wine in the United States has led to some cunning plans for the exploitation of its popular success.

### EUROPE: A BACKGROUND

Although there are many local variations, the buying and selling of wine in Europe can be reduced to three simple cases, which are offered here by way of background to the American trade:

*First Case*
The grower sells his grapes or his wine in barrels to a producer who is responsible for vinification and/or bottling, and who takes full credit for the wine on the label. Sale of the wine is normally direct to the U.S. importer, or through the action of an agent. Such wines are mostly regional.

*Second Case*
Here, the same grower may sell his grapes or his un-bottled wine to a shipper who will bottle the wine, take credit for it on the label, and arrange for its widespread distribution without an agent. The wine will normally be sold to a major U.S. importer as of regional or more precise origin.

*Third Case*
This is the only situation in which the grower is not anonymous. He makes his own wine—although does not necessarily bottle it—and attaches his name to the label. His product may be purchased by a shipper for distribution, or its sale may be arranged by an agent. Alternatively it may be sold directly to the American importer.

## THE DISTRIBUTION NETWORK

Our current system of legislation with regard to the sale and consumption of alcoholic beverages exists, in all its complexity, as a result of attempts to enforce the strictest controls after the repeal of prohibition in 1933. At the federal level, the Bureau of Alcohol, Tobacco and Firearms has authority to control the labeling and nomenclature of all wines sold in the United States, and to impose restrictions on the manufacture and content of domestic wines. At the state level, the situation is less clear. In some eighteen states the trading of liquor is a state monopoly, with the principles of the liquor laws often applied to the control of wine. In one state, prices may be fixed and subject to approval, while in others the whole business of alcohol might be as loose as it is in certain parts of Europe. This confusing situation has led to the existence of what are really three basic channels of distribution:

## 1) Traditional

Here, the importer buys his wine from abroad, stores it in his own warehouse, then sells it to a regional wholesaler at a profit. The wholesaler in turn sells it to the retailer who imposes his own mark-up before it is sold to you. The importer in this case is often a major liquor company, whose products are vital merchandise in the majority of wholesale and retail operations. The opportunities for the exertion of pressure on the buyer to carry the importer's basic wines in return for liquor distribution rights are obvious. The traditional, three-tier system, however, does offer certain advantages by virtue of its structural stability.

## 2) The Broker System

The broker, or agent system originates in a desire to bypass the traditional network. Here, the distributor becomes the importer, and the agent simply arranges the sale from the exporter abroad, often on an exclusive basis. The agent, it should be noted, has no inventory at any time. Such a system questions the otherwise monolithic status of the traditional importer. During the great wine glut of the early '70s it became the operational vehicle of certain less reputable organizations, which more or less died when the market stabilized.

### 3) *The Direct Import*
Its title is deceiving, since the system is actually indirect. A major retailer makes informal plans for the shipment of wines for his own use, and asks a wholesaler to arrange clearance. Since the distinction between the direct import and the special order has never been clear, the system, under stable circumstances, would seem both legal and healthy. (We should point out that, except in a few isolated cases, it is illegal for the retailer to import his wine directly. Bulk importation by individuals is federally prohibited.)

What is possibly the single, most distressing problem facing today's trade is the issue of transportation and storage. Although the larger, more reputable companies are in a position to ship their wines in refrigerated containers, this impressive arrangement can break down completely once the wine is warehoused. It is a common complaint of European producers that their wines cannot be fairly judged when subjected to violent extremes of temperature when they get to America. If one considers the shipping route from Rotterdam to Miami, the argument becomes awfully real. To make matters worse, the majority of American distributors are sadly equipped for temperature-controlled storage, while the exporters themselves are often slack in monitoring conditions on their own docks. The problem is compounded by the increasing frequency of "treatment" during vinification in order to counteract the problem by rendering the wines insensible to ambient conditions. (Whether or not such products still deserve to be called wine is debatable.) As consumers, we have no choice in this matter but to rely on the reputation and integrity of our better merchants.

THE STREAMLINING OF THE AMERICAN TRADE

If it were not for the action of certain serious retailers and the equally serious customers they serve, we would probably not see any exceptional wines at all in this country. To the distributor they are a nuisance. They cannot be sold in supermarkets, they are too highly priced for a mass market, and they tie up too much precious capital in inventory. What is worse, the majority of salesmen who represent the wholesaler know very little about wine and are in no position to discuss the relative subtleties of quality estates. The wholesaler generally wants his business to be as simple as possible, preferably restricted to bulk items that do a volume (or at least predictable) business: hence a trend towards domestic jug wines, which are easy to understand and easy to sell, or, in the case of imports, a brand name.

The brand name, in most areas of consumption, is one of the most remarkable phenomena peculiar to the western world. It all starts with advertising and the security of a highly promoted, nationally distributed product. Those that are successful are very successful and they have made a lot of money for everyone involved. It is obvious that wine is a very real mystery to the majority of American consumers. The brand name people understand this, but prefer it to stay that way.

A successful brand name product is usually the result of some very careful thought. Its taste is designed to be entirely inoffensive and to be appropriate to most foods and social situations. Its name is memorable and easy to pronounce, and its packaging instantly recognizable. It is either an effort to exploit the popularity of some element of wine that is universally appealing, or it is created to be identified only by its name with no regard to its vinification or origin. It claims to offer consistent quality and removes the need for vintage familiarization. In short, what it is selling is safety, comfort, and confidence. Since its distribution is of paramount importance it relies largely on the traditional three-tier system to overcome local structural variations and is normally associated with a preestablished and comprehensive distribution network, often through the liquor business.

It has done three things. First, it has significantly helped popularize the consumption of wine. Secondly, it has, in certain cases, introduced consumers to some of the delights of the wines of a particular area. Thirdly, it has charged the customer for the above services. Since great wines cannot be mass produced, it follows that the brand-name product can never be more than a common denominator. It is generally true that such wines, which do not refer to a precise and limited geographical area, can never be of exceptional quality. Brand name wines are never bad—they cannot afford to be, but it is worth considering two factors with regard to wine

THE COSTING OF THE CLASSIC BOTTLE

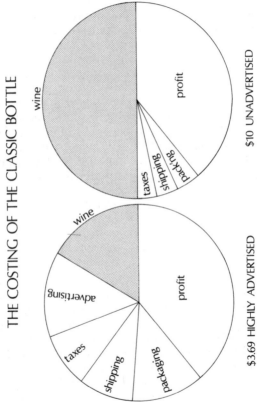

$10 UNADVERTISED

$3.69 HIGHLY ADVERTISED

advertising on a large scale. First, who pays for it? Secondly, what is the nature of the advertisement: does it explain the quality of the product, or does it present itself in much the same way as just another marketable item competing for a market share?

## THE RETAIL STORE

There are really two types of retail stores that take wine seriously. Since both serve the consumer in different ways, we will take them as separate cases.

The first is the large, all-purpose store which will probably advertise itself as offering large discounts, and special offerings in the fashion of a food supermarket: it will frequently be a part of a larger chain of similar stores. It does indeed have the advantage of superior buying power, which often leads to the passing on of those discounts to the consumer level. It is unfortunately at the mercy of its buyer who is normally responsible for the purchasing policies of the entire chain. His selections can be good and interesting and intelligently placed in those stores located in the more selective areas of major markets; in which case, the volume profits from the main part of this chain, normally from liquor, brand name and popular items, will be used to offset the cost of offering an impressive selection of wine in his "serious" stores at decent prices. Because of the size of his market, he is usually in a position to offer a wide array of secondary services in the form of wine clubs and tastings. Such advantages, however, are both highly structured and limited. Unfortunately, he is anonymous: you may never meet the buyer and will in most circumstances deal with a clerk or cashier who is probably in no position whatsoever to give you any advice as to the nature of your purchase. Furthermore, because of the volume nature of his trade, he is mostly concerned with buying established, safe names, and his inventory may be slightly limited in that direction. Essentially, buying from the volume store presupposes considerable knowledge of the market on the part of the serious consumer. Decidedly not a place for the beginner, or he may end up buying the brand name from the floor display.

The small store that offers a wide selection of good wines is probably independently owned, or part of a strictly limited group. Here you will meet the owner almost anytime, and herein lies the shop's principal advantage. Although secondary services are probably more limited than in the large chain, the buyer-seller relationship can be very personal indeed. If you find the right place, you may be able to learn a lot about wine in a very short space of time. The breadth of selection will probably be roughly similar to the chain store, but with a greater emphasis on interesting, often obscure buys than on the familiar items. Here the owner is probably also the buyer and is visible behind the counter; he is often very interested in wine, and searches for the unheard-of little gems that will introduce his customers to a genuinely worthwhile wine drinking experience. Storage of wine tends to be better since it is subject to immediate control by the buyer-owner. Although prices may not be the lowest, the small wine shop is principally selling selection, personal service, genuine advice, and care. He is, if you like, a wine merchant in the traditional sense. He is generally buying and selling what he likes, which is quality. Both he and the chain are likely to offer substantial discounts on cases, mixed or otherwise.

It is of course entirely possible to find the good people in the chain store too, but that is generally not, by virtue of the structure and size of such a store, where the emphasis normally lies. Unfortunately, just as the independents are the frequent hideouts of affable devotees to the art of wine, so they are also the unfortunate dens of a less pleasant variety of person. It would seem to be axiomatic in all situations that high-pressure salesmanship and sensitivity to the subtleties of wine just do not go together. One occasionally comes across a rather sly form of pressure salesmanship which takes the form of the good-looking, intimidating store, which is actually a front for the sale of bad wine. Such a store is often populated by the fake connoisseur, someone who thinks he has arrived because he knows roughly where Burgundy is on the map. If providence has placed him in the unfortunate position of being responsible for the shop's purchasing, you will probably find that the majority of his inventory consists of impressive labels from unimpressive shippers: strong evidence of a weekly dump by a shrewd salesman from the distributor. It is just possible, however, that he really does know his wines, and knows perfectly well that the majority of his customers buy labels without regard to quality. In this case he will create sales—specials of

impressive looking names selling for impossibly
low prices. Check the label very closely indeed: you
will probably find the wine to be a subtly laundered
fake, in fact rank deception.

Some sales, we would hasten to point out, are entirely genuine and laudable. Find out how the wine
got there. Occasionally it will be the result of a
dump by the distributor, perhaps in bankruptcy
situations, or as the occasional result of a genuine
desire to promote the wine for a limited period at
reduced prices. (In all sale situations we would
make the immediate recommendation that you
never, unless you are absolutely certain of what you
are buying, commit yourself to more than a single
bottle.) Another type of sale is the pre-sale, where
the serious retailer puts together a list of important
wines, and offers them to his regular customers on
an advance order basis, thereby forming a sizable
order, which he can present to the distributor: such
sales are normally worked out ahead of time with
the distributor's cooperation, and done simply
because the retailer believes in what he is doing,
and is concerned with good customer service. Here
is a person who will sell you an inexpensive Mâcon
Blanc from a good shipper rather than an expensive
Pouilly-Fuissé from a poor one: he knows that
popular name wines are subject to abuse and over-
pricing, and is able to point to wines from neighboring districts, often of excellent quality, but without
the big name. Thus he saves you money, and you
come back for more.

Possibly the most repugnant of all the creatures
you will encounter behind the counter is the im-

possible snob. He will assume you are an idiot, and
feel it his duty to punish you for your ignorance.
You will either walk away feeling intimidated and
never buy another bottle of wine as long as you live,
or you will have bought an immature classified
growth, which is both beyond your budget and not
exactly appropriate for tomorrow's picnic. He is
normally distinguished by the lack of any obvious
skeletal structure, and an unhealthy preoccupation
with dust.

## SPECULATION AND VALUE

In the early 1970s something very peculiar—and
hopefully never to be repeated—happened to the
American wine market. Basically it boomed. Grasp-
ing the massive increase in sales and interest in
wine, the American trade and consumer suddenly
realized that here money was to be made. More
people seemed to be drinking wine, and prices were
certainly going steadily up. The consequence was a
massive investment in anything that called itself
wine. The market was literally flooded. Rash
purchases of poor quality wines were made by im-
porters, and the distribution network began to
break down. Wines which might have been entirely
adequate in the locales of their origin just did not
make it comfortably to the States. Along with that
there were a number of major political scandals in
the French wine trade, which exposed certain shippers as dealing in fraudulent practices—and the
wines were right here on our doorstep, if not in our

warehouses, homes or, even worse, our gullets. The bottom dropped right out of the market, and a lot of companies and individuals were left with huge stocks of unsalable wine. To make matters worse, the country entered an economic recession and all those expensive classified growths, German estates and big Burgundies were now firmly excluded from the nation's budget. The final outcome was a dump of unprecedented scale of imported wines at silly prices, good wines mixed in with bad. This upset the European producers, who were no longer able to sell to America on a consistent basis, and they went elsewhere to explore new markets in Switzerland, Belgium, and Sweden. The effects are still there, although the market has now roughly regained its stability.

Lesson: do not speculate in wine unless you really know what you are doing. If your purchase is "safe" (classified Bordeaux, for instance), and you intend to drink the wines you are investing in at some point in the future (when their prices will hopefully have increased considerably), then you are probably being sensible. If, however, you are buying in the hope of selling your wines at a profit, then you are very misguided. To whom exactly will you sell your Moutons and Richebourgs? You almost certainly do not have the contacts in the trade who might be able to use your stocks, and you definitely do not have a license. Buy only for yourself and preferably stay with the most predictable and tried of estates.

Value in wine is an elusive and amorphous quality. We probably know more about where it does not lie than where it does. Unless you wish to succumb to those national advertising strategies, in which case these words are wasted, it does not often lie in brand name products. It lies in the products of some shippers, but with major reservations with regard to others. It certainly lies in inexpensive jug wine, if you like inexpensive jug wine. Value in wine lies most often in wines of specific, limited regions (and not necessarily the most famous), which have been made by a man who is identified on the label and who does only what he has always done, no more no less. It is wine honestly made and honestly sold. Its price is reasonably stable, and is directly related to the quality of the product. It never comes cheap, in the worst sense of that word, but comes fairly, with no excuses. It is good and clean, and precisely what you paid for. It is wine.

Finding real wine is not difficult: there is plenty to be had, in return, if you wish, for the most modest of sums. It requires a little time and intelligent awareness. Its name is integrity. If you find it at your merchant's, it can probably be traced all the way back through the distribution network to the neatly trimmed vines in some simple vineyard.

## FRAUD

Fraud has been with the wine business since man first traded the substance. It takes many forms, most of them, happily, not of domestic origin. Federal law generally protects the origins and appellation of foreign products in so far as they are protected in their country of origin. Certain appellations, however, are not protected in the United States when considered to be of a non-specific generic nature rather than statements of source: extended to include, for example, Rhine, Champagne, Chablis, Burgundy, and Sauternes. Such appellations tend, however, to be protected with regard to their false adoption by other European countries, and as such are prohibited in this country.

Within Europe, the situation is confusing. Local laws attempting to regulate the manufacture, labeling, and sale of local wines often exist in apparent contradiction to the general wine laws of the European Economic Community, a matter that has become the subject of much current debate in the trade. Yet laws do exist, which are fundamentally concerned with the protection of consumer rights and the integrity of the wine trade. They are enforced, but only as far as they can be enforced. Most vintners' cellars are strangely anonymous, barrels often identified only by chalked-in codes, and labels are not attached to bottles until they are ready to be sold. It is increasingly true, certainly in France and Germany, that wines are no longer adulterated with substances other than wine: in Germany in particular, the law has been created very intelligently so that the vintner has legal means at his disposal to make acceptable wines on a yearly basis without infringing the law. Beware, however, of wines with German-looking labels that are made outside Germany and beyond governmental control: a situation that applies to popular name items for export. In France, the prosecution of fraud has seemed at times to be of a distinctly political nature. We hear more about fraud in Burgundy than we do in Bordeaux. But Burgundy is a fragmented rural society, quite unlike Bordeaux, which is a much more homogenous community of wine makers, focused in the City of Bordeaux—which, as one eminent Bristol shipper likes to point out, has sixty thousand votes. Here, there is rarely a surplus of wine.

But go to Burgundy, take a look at one of those famous communes and ask yourself, where does all that wine come from? Note also in Bordeaux that several important growths also own, or are intimately related to a minor château: how does this fare when it comes time to declare how big the harvest was for each, when the value of one is so radically different from the other? Remember that in France the government requires that a statement of what was made by each individual vintner is posted only after he has made it. When fraud does happen these days, it is usually a paper fraud, in other words an agreement between the buyer and the seller that the wine be listed in its documentation as something other than it really is, thus reducing the cost to the buyer, while retaining the wine theoretically in the inventory of the seller. Excess wine to fill empty barrels is never difficult to find. In France there is no requirement that the vintage be stated on the certificate of *Appellation*. In fact it is something of a joke in some parts that wine people keep two sets of records, one for themselves and one for the authorities.

Fraud is not rampant, but it can and does happen, and will continue as long as the market is con-

cerned with buying labels and prices rather than
what is in the bottle. It is frequently a particularly
difficult thing to prove and, like the intervention of
any legal enforcement agency, it is subject to the
fluctuations of the political marketplace. It is further
confirmation that if you want to buy good, genuine
wine, you have to be sure of the person who made
it.


### THE AMERICAN CONSUMER

We discussed earlier in this chapter the American
consumer's susceptibility to national advertising,
which has led to a deep penetration of the wine
market by brand name items. One sometimes won-
ders whether such products would have succeeded
quite so impressively had their marketing strategies
been a little less clever. The dramatic failure of
others seems largely attributable to their inability to
project status, a new and important element in the
game of popular wine.

The Portuguese rosé and Spanish sangria market
has been badly hit: annual sales of Portuguese wines
in the United States decreased by 24% in 1975, and
Spanish wines by 46%. Even more disastrous has
been the rapid decline of the low quality, non-
specific wines manufactured in the United States.
While the consumption of spirits has increased in
this country by 77% since 1960, the increase in wine
sales has almost doubled that (122%). The annual
per capita consumption of wine in 1960 was a little
less than a gallon: in 1976 it was closer to two. It has

been projected that the volume of imported wines will have reached an amazing 132,000,000 gallons per annum by 1990, which would triple the same figures for 1975.*

Essentially, Americans have become more sophisticated in their habits and tastes. The inexpensive, sweetish sparkling wines with pretty colors are no longer as important as they used to be. There has been an enormous trend towards the drier white wines, which satisfies the great American taste for things cold. Much of this is attributable to an increased concern with eating and dining properly, both in the restaurant and at home. Knowledge of wine has become a social grace, and along with it have come the snobbery and pretension—and a growing interest in quality. Americans are relaxing a little.

*"Les vins et spiriteux français au U.S.A." *Revue Vinicole Internationale,* June 1976. Conference, "French Wines and Spirits in the U.S.A.", New York, February 1976.

# Four
# Storing and Serving

WINE is a complex organic substance, and must be handled accordingly. Storage, although critical, is a relatively simple matter and good conditions are well within the reach of most of us.

Essentially, wine needs to sit quietly where it will not be disturbed by any severe changes in the environment until it is ready to be served. A good cellar, which may as well be a closet as a subterranean cavern, is consistently cool, damp, dark and quiet. Although, under ideal circumstances, cellar temperatures should remain within the approximate range of 50°F. to 55°F., wine will survive quite happily at temperatures as high as the sixties or even seventies. More important than coolness, however, is evenness of temperature throughout the year. Dampness is a useful factor in warding off the cork weevil, while darkness is important in preventing the possible occurrence of undesirable photochemical reactions.

Wine, of course, should under no circumstances at any point in its history be shaken or disturbed. Proper maturation requires the absolute stillness of the wine, free even of knocks and local vibrations— this particularly applies to the lower end of the frequency scale. (It has often been observed that a mere five days of trans-Atlantic crossing will frequently age a wine to a point that might otherwise be reached by a year or so of normal aging.) Since tight air seals require wet, expanded corks, bottles should always be stored on their sides: corks *will* dry out and the results *are* disastrous. Again, it is the constancy of the environment that is of absolute importance in the storage of wine.

BEFORE SERVING

We are concerned in this section with wine service in general: the special problems of restaurants are tackled in Chapter Five.

There are three considerations in the treatment of wines before serving: standing, breathing, and temperature. Any wine that has thrown even the lightest sediment should be carefully stood upright for a good two days prior to opening, or for as long a period as possible if notice is short. Actual breathing times will vary with the age and quality of the wine. A very young claret, for instance, which is rich in tannin, will benefit from a full three hours of aeration, while a wine that is particularly mature should probably not be breathed at all. Exposure to the air brings about some degree of rapid oxidation and is useful in bringing the wine to a point of unnatural maturity, often mellowing an otherwise uncompromising product. As a footnote to breathing, it should be added that the process may also remove any whiff of sulfur dioxide that might be present in inexpensive sweet whites, often overdosed to inhibit secondary sugar fermentations. Breathing may also help remove the problem of *bottle stink*, an unpleasant odor associated with deteriorating old wines, but then any new source of oxygen may be too much for a wine in this state of maturity anyway. Decanting (see below) is, of course, the most efficient way of breathing a wine quickly.

Since white wines are significantly more volatile than reds (thus releasing their bouquets more easily), they tend to require not only less breathing time, but can also be served at cooler temperatures. It should be pointed out immediately, however, that the American practice of chilling all liquids to the point of being "good and cold" is in no way desirable for the satisfactory consumption of good white wines. The colder a wine becomes, the less its taste is apparent, particularly the fresh acidity and fruitiness so often associated with white wines. (Unfortunately, it is sometimes true that a wine is so unpleasant that it must be chilled into oblivion, so that no one will ever come to taste or smell its inherent ugliness.) Thirty minutes to an hour in the refrigerator should suffice for a good white, and perhaps even no chilling at all for the best. Ideal serving temperatures fall somewhere between 47°F. and 54°F.

Red wines, on the other hand, need significantly more encouragement than whites in releasing their "flavor" and bouquet. Always serve at room temperature, but preferably no higher than 65°F. At temperatures of 70°F. and above, the alcohol will begin to volatalize and mask the aroma of the wine's other constituents.

Apéritif wines, such as dry sherries or white port, should normally be lightly chilled.

The important principle in controlling temperature when moving wines from the cellar to the table is that the change should be as gradual, or as limited as possible. Ice buckets for this reason are best reserved for sparkling wines or for picnics, where the degree of coldness is preferably maintained at a constant level. Otherwise, ice may be used for a brief period to bring the wine to the desired temperature, after which the bottle should be removed as quickly as possible.

## UNCORKING

A matter of particular fear and apprehension for the novice, uncorking is actually quite simple when handled with a modicum of intelligence and care. Corkscrews come in a variety of forms, most of which do the same job in roughly the same fashion (the exception to the standard spiral corkscrew is the needle opener, which works on a pressure basis and is not recommended). We would suggest that the spiral itself be reasonably long and broad to facilitate a firm, tight penetration of the length of the cork. Furthermore, it should work on some reverse action or lever principle so that the cork may be removed in a slow, straight line. The traditional T-shaped opener is a useful stand-by and frequently offers superior properties in the configuration of the spiral.

Start by cutting the capsule—a soft metal, plastic, or wax seal which covers the upper neck and cork—cleanly below the lip of the bottle. Insert the point of the screw slightly sideways into the center of the cork, then straighten and begin turning. Do not, under any circumstances, push: simply turn until the screw has penetrated the depth of the cork, but no further. When you are sure of a firm grip, pull the cork slowly and gently from the bottle, taking care not to shake the wine. Corks occasionally break off, particularly those classic long specimens from Bordeaux, in which case you must simply start over again, this time, however, screwing towards the side of the bottle to avoid any direct downward pressure that might sink the cork irretrievably. If necessary, penetrate the cork completely to secure your grip. In the case of particularly old and fragile corks, it is useful to have access to a special opener which has no screw at all, but rather two thin, slightly flexible metal blades that grip the cork by its sides.

Champagne and sparkling wines, of course, are entirely different and require, at the outset, a word of warning. Since sparkling wines must be kept under several atmospheres of pressure, the glass that holds them is appropriately strong. But it is not armor. If a sparkling wine is not well chilled, or if it is shaken in any way, it is liable to explode. For this reason, the bottle should always be covered and held with a (white) cloth and handled with intelligence and care. With the base resting against you, take the cork and neck firmly in the left hand, with the bottle pointing diagonally upwards and outwards, well away from persons or items of value. Pull back the wire loop at the base of the cork and untwist, so loosening the wire from the lip of the bottle. Take the base of the bottle in the right hand and twist from the bottom, pulling gradually as you do so. The cork should come out easily, without any pop or the spilling of precious liquid over the room or your guests. Keep the bottle in a diagonal position for a couple of seconds to equalize the pressure, then pour. Opening Champagne is both simple and safe as long as you think of the bottle as a pressurized container.

Sparkling wines should only be "popped" on festive occasions, when the noise adds to the atmosphere of the room. Otherwise, no wine should ever be popped, but opened carefully and silently. This is particularly true of a restaurant situation. For still wines, popping can be avoided by gripping the cork with thumb and forefinger at the last stages of withdrawal.

Once opened, the lip of the bottle should be wiped clean of any mold that has built up on the outside of the cork with a fresh, slightly damp (white) cloth (this type of build-up is quite normal in the case of old red wines). If the bottle is to be recorked for any reason, make sure that the inside goes back into the bottle first (it is cleaner), rewetting it with a little of the wine to help restore the seal. The wine should be poured slowly without allowing the bottle to come into contact with the glass: drips can be taken up by twisting the bottle as you pull it away, then wiping with your cloth, now folded into a neat pad.

GLASSES

Selection of glasses, although not of the highest order of importance, is often desirable to do justice to the particular character of the wine being served, and highly recommended in the case of wines of special quality. Figure Two illustrates some possible variations and describes their potential uses. We feel the all-purpose glass *(a)* is of basic importance and will do quite well if a variety of shapes are not available. At the outset, it is worth stating that a wine glass should be clear in all instances, color being important not only as a criterion for judgment, but also as the first delight in the wine experience.

The all-purpose tulip meets the basic requirements for the majority of occasions. It is clear so that the wine can be seen. It has a stem so that the glass can be held without marring the aesthetics of the visual experience with those greasy fingers that might also warm the wine. It can be used quite satisfactorily for most occasions.

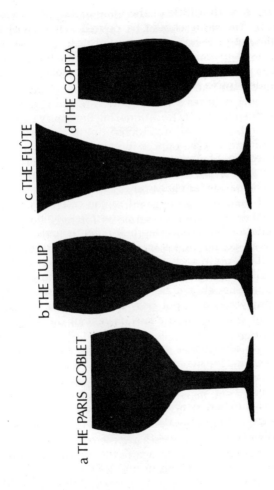

a THE PARIS GOBLET

b THE TULIP

c THE FLÛTE

d THE COPITA

Red wines are the most demanding, since they have the most bouquet to capture. They must be allowed to breathe within the glass, holding the aroma and concentrating it in the nose. It is for this very reason that the glass should never be filled more than half-way. It has been argued that a big bouquet requires a fat container, reaching extreme proportions in the traditional big Burgundy glass. In general, however, the outer limits are probably eight and twelve ounces in capacity. Curved sides are preferable to adequately focus the bouquet.

White wines are less demanding since the bouquet is rarely as big—but should never be ignored since their aroma can be miraculous. Glasses tend to work on the same principle as for reds, but on a smaller scale. Interestingly enough, it is the white wine regions that seem to have produced the greatest variety of local style, ranging from the delicate cut-glass crystal of the Mosel Trier glass to the austere sloping sides of the tasting glass of Anjou.

Champagne and sparkling wines have suffered the greatest of abuses. Central to the Champagne experience is that bubbly delight we call the *mousse*, that often ferocious fizz produced when the carbon dioxide has been released. In the flat saucer glass, so often, alas, referred to as a Champagne glass, it is precisely that *mousse* that will disappear almost immediately. For that reason, a relatively tall, slender glass should be chosen to provide a limited exposed surface area. Ideal glasses are the conical *flûte* from Champagne itself, or again the ubiquitous tulip. Since Champagne and its bubbles are part of a particularly sensual experience, tickling the nose with an expensive prickle, the Champagne glass may be filled a good two-thirds full.

Fortified wines are normally drunk in smaller doses and their glasses are fittingly scaled down. The *copita* from Jerez is an elegant and specialized sherry glass whose slender form chimneys its bouquet into a small opening.

Finally, wine glasses should be washed with only the smallest amounts of mild detergent, rinsed very thoroughly, and polished when still warm. The importance of the glass' absolute neutrality of taste cannot be overemphasized: a visual examination and a good sniff before pouring should serve as adequate safeguards in case of doubt. It should be noted that wine glasses, when used in varying sizes to differentiate wines from each other, are located at the right of the place setting, never more than three at a time, with the first glass on the outside and nearest the guest. A triangular arrangement is often both attractive and convenient.

## DECANTING

Possibly the most mystifying of all the activities of the wine professional is that delicate game of candleflame and balance we call decanting. In actual fact, decanting is just about as simple as pulling a cork, and is a useful, often imperative technique. It serves two purposes: first, to separate clear wine from sediment; and secondly, to breathe young wines. Decanting is the exclusive domain of red and sedimentary fortified wines, particularly old vintage or crusted ports.

Take the uncorked bottle in one hand and the decanter in the other. A candle is placed behind and below the top of the bottle. As you pour from one vessel to the other, you will eventually come to sediment, which will be made visible by the candlelight through the neck: stop pouring and leave the deposit in the bottom of the bottle. The whole process should be as careful and uninterrupted as possible. Under less than ideal circumstances, when the wine has only recently been stood up and the sediment is still in partial suspension, it may be necessary to make several small decantings as the deposit gradually sinks.

# Five
# The Restaurant:
# A Guide to Survival

The restaurant probably represents the ultimate source of fear for the cautious beginner. When faced with an overwhelming list of foreign words, and the prospect of a sommelier who holds the very worst aspects of wine snobbery deep in his sinuses, it is all too easy to fall back on the familiar ill-defined Chablis or something red from California that calls itself Burgundy, the only anchor in a turbulent sea of unspoken wisdoms and knowing glances. But again, like so many aspects of wine, the restaurant situation is easily approached with comfort and confidence so that an otherwise formidable ritual of formality may become the aid to comfort and enjoyment for which it was originally intended.

## THE WINE LIST

We have found that big restaurant wine lists tend to fall into three categories:

### 1) The Plush Plush
On the whole these do not come as too much of a surprise. They are big, and the prices are consistently astronomical. You can expect to spend some money here to buy even the simplest of wines. Under these circumstances, it is mostly foolish to go the whole hog and buy one of those classified Bordeaux from some dusty vintage that you're not sure of anyway. Play safe. Choose something simple and reliable, something from a good shipper of a decent but not exceptional year. But don't go cheap (if that's possible here) since your service may vary accordingly, and the wine will probably be expressly designed for palates of copper. Find what seems like a good, unpretentious deal and be prepared for the bill.

### 2) The Fake Plush
This is possibly both the least agreeable and also most common list, put together by a man who is only marginally less oily than his salad dressings. Here the prices are more or less acceptable, but the wines beyond the realms of drinkability: either good-looking names from terrible shippers, bad years, or both; or impressive labels with equally impressive prices of vintages that won't be ready for another decade. Whoever put this one together is quite convinced that you possess neither perception

nor sense. Stick with beer and hope for decent food.

*3) The Good List*
These, alas, are rare findings, but when they do
show up they are marvelous and you are a customer
forever. This is the list of a quality establishment,
put together with genuine wine knowledge and
sensitivity to the customer's tastes with regard both
to price and quality. There is usually a balanced
selection of good wines that cross the spectrum of
sound drinkability. Sommeliers are even helpful
here and often in a position to make sensible recommendations. The proprietor will probably make his
living by offering pleasant domestic house wine at a
high mark-up to offset a lower profit margin on his
better wines. Since the wine list is frequently an indicator of the rest of the establishment, you can expect to have an enjoyable evening. If you want to
try a truly great wine in a restaurant situation, this
is certainly the time to do it.

### THE DECISION

Having determined the nature of the list you are
faced with, feel out the other members of your party
with regard to general considerations of taste, and
then form a consensus of choice in terms of menu
selections for each individual course. Certain foods
will require certain wines, the principles of which
are discussed in Chapter Seven. Some sort of com-
promise, however, may be necessary when dishes

differ radically from guest to guest. If you intend to order a different wine with each course, it is worth letting your intentions be known at the time of the initial order. This will help assure the party of some sort of coordination of service, and allow wines to be prepared as the situation requires. Certainly, if a wine to be served later in the meal is to be stood or breathed, it is advisable to ask that the bottle be opened immediately, a consideration that is not always taken for granted. Dessert wines should not be ordered until the meal is over, and then only when the rest of the party has shown sufficient interest: some may have drunk enough, or may prefer to go straight into a Cognac or liqueur.

It is customary in Europe to order wine not by name, but by the number as it appears on the list. This procedure has much to recommend it: not only does it prevent embarrassment, even confusion, from the mispronunciation of names, it can also allow for speedier service since the number on the list is usually the number of the storage bin in the restaurant's cellar.

An understanding of the effects of temperature on wine is important and has been fully discussed in the previous chapter.


THE SOMMELIER

The best way of approaching the whole issue of the presentation of your wine is to take a look at roughly how it *should* be done.

Service of wine and other beverages is always

from the customer's right: since food is served from the left, this gives the restaurant staff the opportunity to work smoothly together. The sommelier presents the wine unopened to the head of the table. This is actually quite important: in certain less reputable establishments, the wine steward might have neglected to tell you that he is now serving a substitute vintage or label—so check it to see that your order corresponds with what you are being served. Ideally, he will repeat the name and vintage of the wine so that all may be easily seen to be correct. Assuming the presentation is acceptable, make some gesture of assent so that the sommelier may proceed to the opening of the bottle.

The bottle should be opened silently and efficiently, always in full view of the head of the table. When the cork has been pulled, the wine will be offered as an ounce or two poured into your glass for approval. (The sommelier will often carry a shallow tasting cup, called a *tastevin*, in which case he may pour a little for himself.) There is much show associated with the inspection of corks, ranging from twisting and breaking to sniffing and even biting, all of which are, to a great extent, meaningless. Certainly, the cork should smell of wine and not of cork, but even if there are problems they will be obvious from your first sniff of the wine in the glass. We do know that if the cork is long and firm, then the vintner has probably spared little expense in the other aspects of his wine making—he apparently cares. But as a magical indicator of the quality of the wine you are about to encounter, it is almost entirely useless. The cork is an afterthought, not a critical preliminary.

Take the glass by base or stem and swirl the wine a little to help release the bouquet. Sniff—but do not (as with the cork) assume that the acceptance or rejection of the wine should be based entirely on that one experience. Then take a good sip to "taste." Remember always the limitations of the wine you have ordered and the circumstances under which it is being judged: has it breathed enough; has it settled after a short standing time? Evaluate the wine purely on what it should be—certainly don't return your Bordeaux Supérieur on the grounds that it doesn't taste like an Haut-Brion.

Now several things could possibly happen, only one of which is just cause for sending the wine back: 1) the wine is acceptable; 2) the wine is acceptable but just a little disappointing—tell the wine steward how you feel since it may provide him with important information for future purchases; 3) the wine is genuinely bad, in which case you must refuse it, preferably politely. In many instances the sommelier will want to taste it himself, which is entirely acceptable. Whatever the verdict (and normally you will be in complete agreement if the wine is truly bad), he will get you another bottle at no additional charge, or offer you the option of trying something else.

Let us assume the wine is good. You have taken your taste and nodded approval, thereby accepting the bottle. The sommelier will pour the wine for your guests and come back to you, using his cloth to wipe the lip of the bottle in each instance. Although in most restaurant situations it is the responsibility of the waiter or sommelier to keep glasses filled, there are times when this just does not happen, in which case it is up to you to do the honors. Serve ladies first, then men, always clockwise around the table, ending up with yourself. If distance is too great, you may wish to have glasses passed to you in the appropriate order, or, in particularly informal situations, pass the bottle around. Throughout the procedure, the wine steward will have made it a point to keep the label visible, finally laying the bottle to rest on your right, again with the label pointing in your direction.

Remember always that these occasions are supposed to be enjoyable. If the sommelier does make the mistake of breaking the cork it may not be his fault: corks are sometimes very tricky indeed. Bear with him—he will probably appreciate any relief from that embarrassment. If you feel it appropriate to tip the sommelier when distinct from the waiter, it is probably best to leave your waiter a generous gratuity and tactfully suggest that they divide it between them. If the atmosphere of the house is particularly casual, the offering of a glass of your wine is often an appreciated gesture.

# Six
# The "Taste" of Wine

THE experience of taste (known technically as
*gustation*) is strictly limited to the sensations of the
tongue, and as such represents only a small part of
the complex procedures that constitute the evaluation of wine. "Tasting" a wine—or, more correctly,
evaluating its quality—requires a complete examination of the physical properties of the product,
commencing with a thorough visual and aromatic
inspection before the experience of what happens
in the mouth is considered.

Although "taste" is, by its very nature, an entirely
subjective experience, certain objective criteria are
both appropriate and necessary to any useful discussion of a wine's quality. Unfortunately, unlike
the raw materials of the visual arts or music, we
cannot point to each specific attribute, touch it or
reproduce it, and say that that is a Corinthian col-
umn, or this a chord: we have to open a bottle,
often of contrived simplicity, and sit around and
communally sniff. There is no short cut to the art of
wine "tasting". We must collect information intelligently, and constantly relate that information
back to the source it seeks to describe.

Luckily, the vocabulary we use is not totally
obscure. Concepts of bitterness or softness, for example, are meaningful almost immediately: they
are part of the highly suggestive vocabulary of
"taste", statements of how we feel about the wine,
quite distinct from the objective properties we can
identify in the wine itself. It is important, therefore,
to keep in mind at the very beginning the distinction between the object of perception and the perception itself. Hopefully, when the wine is right,
they will all come together in one coherent whole,
but if we cannot separate the parts we shall never
know when the wine is wrong. It is the difference
between looking at the Parthenon and thinking it
nice, and coming back after reading a book about art
and finding it brilliant. All we need is a little intelligent curiosity, and we are on the threshold of a
whole new world.

In this chapter, we are concerned with the five

basic aspects of evaluation, with a brief explanation
of the vocabulary needed at each point.

FIRST ASPECT: VISUAL

Attempt as far as possible to examine the wine in a
source of clear white light: daylight is ideal, but not
always practicable; all forms of artificial light are
acceptable, but each in its own way is unfair to certain parts of the visible spectrum, making some colors more or less visible than they actually are.
Candlelight has a strongly romantic appeal, but is
usually sufficiently dim as to prevent differentia-
tion of subtleties in hue. Get to know the limitations
of your light source, and work the best you can with
it. It is more or less imperative to have available a
white surface against which the wine may be examined—a tablecloth is ideal. (Needless to say, the
glass should be clear.)

There are really two parts to the visual aspect:
color and physical properties, both of which are important. Color is an immediate stimulus. White
wines will vary from the palest of flaxen yellow,
through the spectrum of yellowness, occasionally
with traces of green, to the deep, golden browns of
aged sweet wines, once rich in tannin. Certain
grapes produce wines of distinctice colors, which
become consistently obvious the more experienced
one becomes. In the case of rosés, little need be said
except that they should tend towards the paler side
of pure pink: any departure from that rule of thumb
could point to sloppy vinification or even more

doubtful practices. With red wines, color is of paramount importance and subject to extensive change. The pigmentation of red wines is, of course, the result of the reaction of tannins and anthocyanins as discussed in Chapter Two. In general terms, particularly young wines are a deep, vivid red, often with traces of purple around the edges. As tannic wines age, the red pigmentation precipitates out, and the color changes to a paler, less intense red, browning around the edges as the wine oxidizes: this will become particularly evident if the glass is tilted on its side so as to reduce the density of the liquid. In extreme cases of brownness, it should be assumed that the wine has reached a stage of fragility and may therefore have to be consumed almost immediately before rapid oxidation pushes the wine forcefully into the realms of senility.

So there are really two elements in the consideration of color: the tint of a wine, and its depth. Some low-tannin wines will show strong signs of youthful pigmentation, but be almost entirely lacking in depth: it can be assumed with some degree of certainty that these wines will be as light in the mouth as they appear in the glass. In no way should this necessarily be interpreted as a statement of badness, only an indication of a possible short life, and a reference to vinification and style.

Having examined the wine's color, we are concerned now with the physical properties of the wine as they are visible. It is generally true that a well-made wine is free of cloud: if it has been fined and filtered in the appropriate fashions, there is no reason for the appearance of any material in suspension. The only instance in which cloudiness might be justified would be in the case of old reds that have begun to throw a fine precipitate. In the early stages of the formation of sediment, the particles have not yet reached a stage where they can settle comfortably at the bottom of the bottle. Rather they remain for a period of time suspended in the body of the wine as a fine cloud: such a departure from absolute clarity is entirely acceptable. It is the direct result of the precipitation of coloring matter, and will occur quite naturally with bottle age and associated color change. Otherwise, cloudiness these days is almost certainly indicative of bacterial spoilage and other misadventures. Examine too the *disk*, or surface, of the wine, which should be absolutely clean and free of any abnormalities.

Next, swirl the wine around the glass, tilt it heavily on its side, and return it to an upright position. The wine will often form a broad surface film, which will fall back down the side of the glass, separating into distinct trails, known as *legs*. Amerine & Roessler have pointed out that the phenomenon is the result of a surface tension/gravity effect, and that the legs are composed almost entirely of water.[*] It would seem to be a direct function of the alcohol content of the wine, and has nothing whatsoever to do with glycerol, as has frequently been stated in the literature. It should not be taken as a statement of quality.

[*]See Bibliography with regard to Amerine & Roessler's excellent study, *Wines: Their Sensory Evaluation*.

### ADDITIONAL TERMS

*Brilliant.*
The superlative of *clear:* the wine is entirely transparent; *clean.*
The opposite of *cloudy.*

*Brown.*
The color, especially around the edges, of an old, *oxidized* red
wine. Caused by the precipitation of pigments, especially tannins. Normally accompanied by sediment. *Bricked* would
describe the same phenomenon at an earlier stage.

*Maderized.*
A state of advanced oxidation in white wines, producing a
brownish color, and *baked* aroma. Considered a fault, except in
certain fortified wines and, in a rather special sense, the *vins
jaunes* of the Jura.

### SECOND ASPECT: SMELL

Smell is central to the evaluation of wine, and occurs both from the familiar action of sniffing, and
also from within the mouth when we breathe out.
In fact, the basis of our experience in the mouth is
not tasting at all, but rather the result of odor perception during exhalation. Smell (technically referred to as *olfaction*) is perceived in a region above
and behind the nose called the *olfactory bulb*, accessible through the obvious route of the nasal
passages, and also through a channel at the back of
the mouth. Odorous stimuli reach the olfactory
region when the air in which they are contained
passes across it.

Breathe out, bury your nose in the glass, and take a quick, strong sniff. Think about it away from the glass, and wait for a short while until your olfactory senses are ready to start again (a second sniff immediately following the first will have decreased in intensity). Next, give the wine a good swirl to increase the surface area and release any final traces of odor. Sniff again.

We should make clear at the outset that there have been numerous definitions of the distinctions between *aroma* and *bouquet*: it is our opinion that most are spurious. An aroma would seem to cover the entire range of a wine's odor, while bouquet refers more specifically to the experience derived from sniffing alone, and is normally applied to aromas of an attractive and powerful nature.

If the wine contains off aromas, they tend to be obvious very quickly. *Sulfur* is often the first to be detected. In general, the younger and more acidic the wine (and this is especially true of whites), the greater the potential for free sulfur dioxide. There is a multitude of other unpleasant smells, largely associated with inadequacies of the vinification process and subsequent bacterial spoilage. For some reason, it has become customary to label a number of variable, non-descript odors as *corked,* possibly because the damaged cork is an easily attributable cause. Genuinely corked wines, however, are quite rare, although immediately indentifiable: wine will penetrate poor corks and form a mold, which in turn gives its own aroma back to the wine. The smell of *sauerkraut* is an instant and unequivocal sign of a poorly controlled malo-lactic fermentation

(see Chapter Two), which will be frequently compounded by the presence of noticeable carbon dioxide in still wines. The list of off odors is endless, and
we are not concerned here with a tabulation of their
types and causes. Let us simply remind ourselves
that they are invariably a sign of poor vinification,
spoilage, or both.

In the case of the good bouquet, however, we are
less interested in identifying the compounds of
which it is comprised. We are conscious instead of
the special qualities of the grape, often released by
the action of fermentation. It is these that are the es-
sence of the bouquet. Specific vinification odors will
frequently hide the basic properties of bouquet on a
temporary basis, often unpleasantly in the form of
*bottle sickness*. (The scientific process whereby bouquets are produced, and under what conditions, is
discussed in Chapter Two.) Ultimately, the bouquet
is a subtle, often spectacular thing, requiring not
only the right quality of raw materials, but also an
exceptional skill on the part of the wine maker in
determining those factors that will both create and
isolate it. Once more, it is balance that is the key to
good wine.

ADDITIONAL TERMS

*Aftertaste.*
Any lasting sensation, not limited to aroma. Subject to enormous
variation in quality and intensity.

*Flowery.*
The aroma of specifically young wines, mostly white.

*Foxy.*
The aroma of Eastern American native grapes, species *Vitis labrusca* (the Fox-Grape). Has no roots in the animal kingdom.

*Fresh.*
The specific aroma of young wines, normally complimentary in the sense of *cleanness*.

*Fruity.*
The aroma of the fruit, i.e., the grape, normally associated with youth.

*Green.*
The aroma of unripe grapes.

*Musty.*
A very unclear term, apparently associated with unpleasant odors.

*Nose.*
Synonymous with *aroma; smell.* Can be good or bad.

*Vinegary.*
The unpleasant aroma of acetic acid, the active constituent in vinegar. Indicative of spoilage.


## THIRD ASPECT: TASTE

Before considering what taste is, we have to decide on what it is not. Once the wine is in the mouth, it quickly warms to body temperature, causing the volatalization of odorous constituents. As we breathe out, these are transported back up to the olfactory region where we experience them as smell. Thus we must be particularly careful not to confuse the stimuli and experience of smell with the limited area of taste.

To all intents and purposes, the phenomenon of taste is the exclusive result of stimuli to the tongue. Different areas of the tongue are sensitive in different ways: *sweetness* at the front, *acidity* along the upper sides, *saltiness* along the lateral edges, and *bitterness* at the back. Since *saltiness* is of almost no importance in the evaluation of wine, we shall ignore it. *Sweetness* is an obvious experience, and is due largely to the presence in the wine of the principal grape sugars, glucose and fructose. (It is interesting, as Amerine & Roessler have pointed out, that the ability to detect sweetness differs considerably from one person to another, apart from enormous variations in the level of personal preference.) *Acidity* is more or less synonymous with *sourness*. *Bitterness* is one of the most confusing sensations of all since it resembles *astringency*, which has nothing to do with taste—that is especially true in the case of substances such as tannins, which are both bitter and astringent.

Having agreed that we are all a little confused at this stage of the game, we might as well give in to the obvious and take a big mouthful, with all its array of aromas. Swirl the wine forcefully around every part of the mouth. Open slightly and, while resting the upper front teeth against the lower lip, draw in air through the small gap between the two. Close once more and continue to swirl and chew to bring the wine into contact with every part of the palate. The air causes a break-up of the wine and allows the aromatic elements to penetrate more easily back up towards the olfactory bulb. This rather noisy process is actually quite acceptable in serious wine circles, but may require some slight modification in polite society.

## ADDITIONAL TERMS

*Balanced.*
Its literal meaning is mostly applied to the relationship of sugar-acid. Otherwise it probably represents one of the most desirable wine attributes, which is the *harmony* of parts.

*Dry.*
Quite simply, not *sweet.*

*Hard.*
Of *uncompromising acidity* and *bitterness.* A safe phrase if you can't be more precise.

*Tart.*
A less assertive version of *sour* or *acidic,* normally applied to young whites.

## FOURTH ASPECT: TACTILE

Tactile sensations in wine are extremely important: we talk about them constantly, often failing to realize just what they are. We are talking here about sensations felt in the mouth, but certainly not limited to the tongue. *Effervescence* is an obvious tactile quality, as is *astringency.* Most important of all, the phenomenon of *body*—of *fullness*—is to a great extent tactile, and, like legs (which are looked at rather than tasted), is a function of the ethanol content of the wine. Alcohol, in fact, is also responsible for the *burning* attributes of many wines. Sugar is important in contributing to the *viscosity (thickness)* of the wine, as is to a limited extent, glycerol. Astringency is confusing for the reasons we stated in the previous chapter.

## ADDITIONAL TERMS

*Heady.*
Synonymous with *alcoholic.*

*Rough.*
Generally refers to wines whose sole advantage is their *alcohol* content.

*Soft.*
A generally pleasant *balance,* suggesting low *tannin* and *acidity.*

*Spritzig.*
A pleasant, slight *effervescence* characteristic of the finer, more delicate wines of Germany.

*Thin.*
Low in *alcohol.* Opposite of *full-bodied.*

## FIFTH ASPECT: GENERAL IMPRESSIONS

Having given some detailed consideration to the objective evaluation of wines, we will hopefully not lose sight of the fact that the wine is there to be enjoyed. It is important to decide throughout our examinations just how we feel about the wine. Do we like it? Is it better or worse than another bottle? What are our reservations? Be honest with yourself, and try to develop a consistent and personally meaningful vocabulary. You may wish to assign a scoring system for each of the facets we have described as an aid to evaluation. But, as we stated earlier, there is really no short cut to learning the faculties of "taste": like all exercises in criticism, they must be researched and practiced. Although some people are taste blind, the areas of their blindness do not normally relate to the composition of wine. Understanding the mechanism of taste is important to anyone with an interest in wine, and, with a little care, is well within our reach as a pleasant and gratifying experience.

## ADDITIONAL TERMS

Almost all the terms that relate to our general sense impressions are of a highly suggestive nature. They are concerned with our overall feelings about a wine, or they represent a synthesis of our objective judgement. They range from *big, balanced,* and *delicate* to *mature, mellow,* and *musty.* They are ultimately the province of personal judgement, and should only be used when their meaning is both consistent and clear.

# Seven
# Wine with Food

MATCHING wine with food, and vice-versa, is entirely a matter of common sense. A general rule, which we have emphasized throughout this book with regard to the internal composition of wine, is also entirely applicable to the fundamentals of good dining: whatever our personal preferences, we should never forget the laws of balance. Food is far more obvious than wine in aroma and flavor, and careful thought should be given to the very real possibility of domination. It will be seen that the traditional protocols of the matter are no more than the ordering of common sense principles, genuine and meaningful criteria that have emerged from centuries of experimentation and (often extravagant) experience.

There are very few foods that will not work with some wine. Particularly *hot foods*, such as curries and certain Mexican dishes, whose real pleasure lies in their density of seasoning, are really the domain of beer, or the simplest of inexpensive chilled wine. We would also recommend the exercise of caution with regard to heavily vinegared *salad dressings*. Since the active component of vinegar is acetic acid whose aroma in wine is an unequivocal indication of spoilage, it is hardly sensible to choose foods whose sole advantage is that they contain it.

The meal might be begun with a straightforward dry white wine, suitable to carry one through a broad range of *soups and starters* without stunning the palate. Simple Burgundies are entirely appropriate, as are the drier whites from the Loire. German wines should never be of greater sweetness than a Kabinett, if a good Q.b.A is not available. Dry, lightly chilled sherries (which make excellent apéritifs) are a common alternative for stronger dishes and soups. In the case of the richer *pâtés* or *smoked salmon*, you may require some additional flavor, perhaps a spicy Alsatian or Nahe. Champagne, in many ways, is the ideal wine to start the meal, having sufficient substance to challenge the more substantial starters, while its effervescence will enliven and clean the palate. If you are with a group of liberal drinkers you might take note of the alcohol content of your opening wines, especially if something glorious is to follow. Although the tactile experience of alcohol may be useful in breaking through the complex flavors of certain foods, at this stage it should remain decidedly in the wings.

Simply remember that French and Mediterranean wines tend to be higher in alcohol than Germans, while cocktails are disastrous.

There is very little we can recommend with *fish* other than dry whites. Fish tends to offer clean but delicate tastes, and red wines are just not appropriate. The importance of the fish course within the scope of the meal is obviously a major indicator for the quality of wine that will accompany it. Burgundies again, or a dry Loire would be especially appropriate. For more highly seasoned, Mediterranean style dishes, you might be better off to observe local custom. The highly alcoholic wines of Southern France work particularly well with their charming, colorful inventions.

It is an axiom that all *meats* should be accompanied by dry wines. In the most austere of presentations, the old rule that red wines accompany red meats (beef, lamb, goose, and duck) and that white wines accompany the remainder (pork, veal, chicken, and turkey) probably holds reasonably true, but is far from inflexible. It is the method of cooking and the style of accompanying sauces and seasonings that are really important.

We would unambiguously suggest that *beef* be served only with red wines of the fullest character—Burgundies, Rhônes, big Beaujolais, and substantially tannic clarets. Both lamb and veal do especially well with red Bordeaux. *Pork* tends to be on the fat side and needs the assistance of fruity, acidic wines: if a white is suggested, then a Mâconnais or Graves would be appropriate, while a red would call perhaps for a Beaujolais or a youngish claret.

Simple *chicken* or *turkey* dishes do well with the lighter reds—Bourgeuil or Chinon—while heavy stuffings and roast birds demand Burgundies and clarets. *Goose* and *duck* are a little different since they are heavier in fat and require something substantial to cut through grease and flavor: a classic red or white Burgundy, or one of the bigger Italians would survive impressively.

*Game* tends to be of an intense, powerful flavor, often served with the richest of sauces and jellies. We would generally recommend nothing short of the biggest reds available.

Again, it is the sauces and stuffings, and the wines they might contain that will become a predetermining factor in the selection of wine for consumption. *Brown sauces* seem to like red wines, while *white* or *cream sauces* are most suited to whites. Clearly, the more assertive the dish, the more powerful the wine.

With *desserts* we must be careful. Many of them are so dogmatic in their sweetness that they will destroy almost anything we serve with them. Possibly one of the sweeter Champagnes is the safest bet since those bubbles seem able to survive even the thickest and creamiest of dishes. If you are considering a fine dessert wine, such as a Sauternes or a late-picked German, you may wish to consider serving it alone on account of its special (and expensive) subtleties of taste. If it is to be served, the dessert should be kept absolutely simple, preferably with a base of fruit. Rich chocolate creams would, under these circumstances, have a particularly unpleasant effect on both your wine and your guests. Fruit puddings, especially those heavy delights of an English Christmas, may again require something sparkling to offset their late-dinner substantiality. Iced desserts should be enjoyed alone or with a glass of simple bubbly. The basic rule of service at the end of a large meal is not to kill your guests with stomach bloaters. You may wish to skip a dessert wine altogether and hold out for the Port or Cognac.

Port, especially vintage port, is a regal drink and should never precede even the biggest of table wines. In particularly assertive cases of self-indulgence, it can only be followed by distilled spirits. We would recommend port with just about any *cheese,* especially the classic blue, hard matured, and cream cheeses. For the strongest and best of cheeses—Stilton is the classic example—nothing short of vintage port will suffice. Fresh, non-citrus *fruits* are particularly pleasant with both fortified and dessert wines.

# Reference

# Appendix A
# The Wines of Germany

THE white wines of Germany have met with a growing flurry of international success. They are cleanly refreshing, lightly alcoholic beverages that fit the entire spectrum of drinkability, from regal feasts to country picnics. They are easily affordable, and available in almost any retail store or restaurant. The business of satisfying this enormous market has reached a level of considerable national importance, and has brought with it a system of controls of unprecedented scope. With general regard to consumer protection, a series of laws was enacted in 1971 to closely monitor the production and marketing of German wines, and to establish certain basic standards of professional integrity and industrial competence. To understand the wines of Germany, therefore, is to come to grips with a structure; to grasp an essential logic of classification that is of basic value to the purchasing policies of the critical consumer.

# GERMANY Anbaugebiete

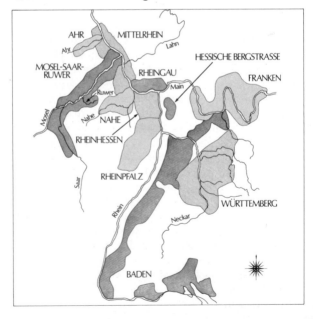

The label is the visible documentation of a wine's pedigree. Apart from providing information with regard to the wine's vintage and producer (which require little explanation), the label must make two important statements that refer to *Place of Origin* and *Quality Level.* Any further description will be little more than a quality-based elaboration of those two basic statements, governed throughout by the fixed standards of German law.

The *Place of Origin* is by far the most important indicator of what the bottle is likely to contain: the more narrowly defined the *Place of Origin,* the better the wine is inclined to be. The identification of a town and vineyard, however obscure, is generally a more valuable guarantee than some vague geographical reference to a river (*Moselblümchen,* for example); or a generic name, such as the highly commercial *Liebfraumilch,* which has almost no geographical implications at all.

There are three *Quality Levels: Tafelwein; Qualitätswein;* and the highest, *Qualitätswein mit Prädikat.* Wines that have been found eligible for this last category are awarded their *Prädikat,* or *title,* on grounds of certain criteria of "taste".

QUALITY LEVELS

*Deutscher Tafelwein*
Table wine, made for everyday consumption. The finished product must be at least 8.5% alcohol, and must be of totally German origin.

*Qualitätswein bestimmter Anbaugebiete (Q.b.A.)*
Wine of a designated region. It must be made of a
"taste" and quality associated with the named
region, and will carry an approval number that has
been assigned by the government for quality control. The 11 designated regions for *Qualitätswein* are
called *Anbaugebiete,* and are as follows:

Ahr
Mosel-Saar-Ruwer             Hessische Bergstrasse
Mittelrhein                  Rheinpfalz
Rheingau                     Baden
Nahe                         Württemberg
Rheinhessen                  Franken

*Verbesserung* (adding sugar to the must) is still permitted. The 8.5% alcohol requirement also applies,
and the wine must, of course, be of German origin.
*Qualitätswein* is also granted the privilege of having
the name of the town, and even the vineyard appear on the label, as long as it complies with the
laws of origin (at least 85% of the grapes to have
originated in the stated vineyard).

*Qualitätswein mit Prädikat*
The term *Pradikat* is literally translated as *title:* so
this is quality wine entitled to a special distinction.
Its origins must be more precisely defined than
those of the simpler *Q.b.A.* The 11 *Anbaugebiete* are
divided into 29 sub-regions, called *Bereiche,* each of
which represents the largest area of cultivation
worthy of a *Prädikat.* In practice, however, *Prädikat*
wines are almost always labeled more presti-

giously—i.e., with town and vineyard names—and the best of these show the name of the producer. Furthermore, if the grape variety is Riesling it is invariably stated in an attempt to bring a better price. The actual *Prädikat* is really a description of the wine's level of sweetness and refers, to some extent, to the timing and selectivity of the vintner at harvest.

There are five possible *Prädikats: Kabinett, Spätlese, Auslese, Beerenauslese,* and *Trockenbeerenauslese. Kabinett* contains the lowest amount of residual sugar of the *Qualitätswein mit Prädikat* level, with *Spätlese* and *Auslese,* increasing proportionately in sweetness. The terms *Auslese, Beerenauslese,* and *Trockenbeerenauslese* progressively imply more specific standards of grape selection. The last two are normally associated with *Noble Rot (Botrytis Cinerea),* which imparts a special complexity to the finished product (the matter is discussed at length in the Sauternes section in Appendix B). Finally, the term *Eiswein* may be added if the grapes were harvested and pressed while their water content was frozen by a late-harvest frost. This concentrates the sugars and acids even more to produce an exceptionally full, sweet wine. In the absence of *Bortrytis,* however, the *Eiswein* will lose much of its remarkable—and expensive—complexity.

## PLACE OF ORIGIN

The legal origins of wines of the *Qualitätswein* level can be stated on the label in a number of ways, becoming generally narrower and more precise as quality improves. To simply mention the *Anbaugebiet,* without further qualification, is to indicate a wine of little more than average quality. Although wines that have been further defined by their *Bereiche* will be of a more distinctive nature than those known only by their *Anbaugebiete,* they are still restricted in quality. Only when the label contains a clear statement of town, vineyard, and (hopefully) producer can a wine begin to represent the finest attributes of a given area—and only here can the full intent of the new law be seen to function.

A listing of important towns follows a discussion of the *Anbaugebiete.* It attempts to note the exceptionally good vineyards of each, and mentions producers who are known for their quality. Some towns are listed twice because their area may cross a dividing line between *Grosslagen.* One *Grosslage,* or vineyard group, may include the production of several towns, while the more specific term, *Einzellage,* refers to an individual parcel of land, which we traditionally associate with a single vineyard. The Mosel-Saar-Ruwer and the Rheingau jointly possess the highest concentration of major names, and they are consequently treated in greater detail.

MOSEL-SAAR-RUWER [1]

1977er [2]

# Zeller [3] Schwartze Katz [4]

QUALITÄTSWEIN [5]

A.P. Nr. 0 000 000 0 00 [6]

Mosel Weinkellerei [7] –Veldenz [8]

---

*Weingut J.L.Wollmann* [1]          *Mittelheim/Rhein* [2]

RHEINGAU [3]

1977er [4]

# MITTELHEIMER [5] SONNENHOF [6]
# RIESLING [7] AUSLESE [8]

Qualitätswein mit Prädikat [9]

*Erzeugerabfüllung* [10]

A.P. Nr. 00 000 000 00 [11]

## THE GERMAN WINE LABEL

*The Regional Wine*
Here the wines of several growers are blended and bottled by a shipper.

1. The *Anbaugebiet:* one of 11 official cultivated regions, which are divided into *Bereiche.*
2. The vintage.
3. The town of origin and association.
4. The *Grosslage:* a collective name for a group of many vineyards within a *Bereich.*
5. The *Quality Level.*
6. The *Prüfungsnummer:* the approval number of the wine, assigned by the authorities for quality control.
7. The identified *Weinkellerei* is the bottler—who is usually also the shipper.
8. The town in which the *Weinkellerei* is located.

*The Estate Wine*
In this case, specific information is stated regarding the wine of a single grower.

1. The *Weingut* is the wine estate, indentified by the owner's name.
2. The town in which the estate is located. Since the estate may hold property in several towns, the statement does not necessarily coincide with the wine's specific origin.
3. The *Anbaugebiet.*
4. The vintage.
5. The town in which the wine was made.
6. The *Einzellage,* or single vineyard of origin.
7. The grape variety.
8. The *Prädikat.*
9. The *Quality Level.*
10. Means bottled by the grower.
11. The *Prüfungsnummer.*

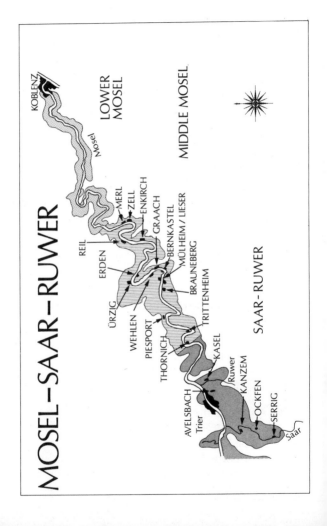

### MOSEL-SAAR-RUWER

The Mosel and its two tributaries, the Saar and the Ruwer, are together responsible for some of the most impressive wines of Germany. Bottled in a brilliant green, they are immediately distinguishable from their brown-glassed neighbors on the Rhine. The Mosel proper is marked by a series of deep bends, formed by hard slate obstructions in the river's course. As vineyard slopes face in the direction of the afternoon sun, so they catch a gentle reflection from the river, warming the slate for chilly evenings. This is a remarkable land, too cool and too far north to enjoy the benefits of a full growing season, and subject to the most sensitive changes in geography and climate.

The business of the area is totally consumed by wine: no other agricultural endeavor is feasible. Even if cold weather crops could survive here—and the soil is so poor it is doubtful—the treacherous hillsides would soon discourage the farmer. Yet the revenues of the better vineyards are sufficiently impressive to have become the sites of some of the most valuable real estate in Germany.

Holdings on the Saar-Ruwer are a little more workable, but still too far north to escape the constant threat of bad weather. Good vintages do not happen often in the Mosel-Saar-Ruwer, but when they do the wines can be very special indeed.

The classic Mosel experience is the clean taste of Riesling—a grape that will provide a special lightness and complexity—and an acid balance that is entirely peculiar to the region. The refreshing acidity of the Mosels is even present in the sweeter *Prädikat* wines, where it is a vital factor in balancing an otherwise isolated richness. The wines gain in drinkability by virtue of their low degree of alcohol. This observation is well understood by certain enthusiastic vintners, in whose cellars the consumption of a single bottle would seem little more than a mouthwash to precede the real business of tasting!

The Saar-Ruwer is separate from the Mosel in flavor, but the differences are very subtle. The soil here is less anonymous than that of the Mosel, and imparts a more mineral quality to its wines. This is possibly more evident in the wines of the Ruwer, but any real distinction can never be more than marginal.

In certain areas, Riesling has been replaced by the more prolific Müller-Thurgau, which provides a higher yield under tough conditions but is less impressive in its overall acidity. Another grape, the Optima, is currently being tried in some good locations, but it is still too early to draw any reasonable conclusions with regard to its quality.

Producers are of particular importance on the Mosel, and the famous names can cost a good deal more than the wines of quality growers with more limited reputations. But do not ignore the famous, nor their prices, since their properties are often the very best, and their superlative quality is both maintained and encouraged by the friendly rivalries of Thanisch, Prüm, and other prestigious estates.

(Exceptional, *e*; very good, *v*; good, *g*.)

ANBAUGEBIET: Mosel-Saar-Ruwer

BEREICH: Zell

TOWN: **Merl**
GROSSLAGE: Schwarze Katz
EINZELLAGEN (VINEYARDS):
Sonneck (*g*)
Königslay-Terrassen (*v*)   Adler (*e*)
RELIABLE PRODUCERS: *Weingut Albert Kallfelz*   Fettgarten (*v*)

TOWN: **Zell**
GROSSLAGE: Schwarze Katz
EINZELLAGEN (VINEYARDS):
Burglay-Felsen (*g*)   Pomerrell (*g*)   Kreuzlay (*g*)
Petersborn-Kabertchen (*g*)   Nussberg (*g*)   Geisberg (*g*)
Domherrenberg (*g*)

Stefansberg (*v*)
Klosterberg (*g*)

BEREICH: Bernkastel

TOWN: **Reil**
GROSSLAGE: vom Heissen Stein
EINZELLAGEN (VINEYARDS):
Goldlay (*v*)   Moullay-Hofberg (*v*)   Falklay (*v*)
Sorentberg (*g*)
RELIABLE PRODUCERS: *R. Müller*

TOWN: **Enkirch** (cont. overleaf)
GROSSLAGE: Schwarzlay
EINZELLAGEN (VINEYARDS):
Edelberg (*g*)   Monteneubel (*g*)   Weinkammer (*g*)
Steffensberg (*v*)   Zeppwingert (*g*)   Herrenberg (*g*)
RELIABLE PRODUCERS: *Winzerverein*

(Exceptional, *e*; very good, *v*; good, *g*)

ANBAUGEBIET: Mosel-Saar-Ruwer

<u>BEREICH: Bernkastel (cont.)</u>

TOWN: **Enkirch** (cont.)
GROSSLAGE: Schwarzlay
EINZELLAGEN (VINEYARDS):
Batterieberg (*v*)                    Ellergrub (*g*)
TOWN: **Erden**
GROSSLAGE: Schwarzlay
EINZELLAGEN (VINEYARDS):
Busslay (*v*)                         Herrenberg (*v*)                    Prälat (*g*)
Treppchen (*e*)
RELIABLE PRODUCERS: *Bischöfliches Priesterseminar, Albert Ehlen-Erben, J.J. Christoffel-Erben (Dr. Her-
mann).*

TOWN: **Ürzig**
GROSSLAGE: Schwarzlay
EINZELLAGEN (VINEYARDS):
Würzgarten (*e*)                      Goldwingert (*g*)
RELIABLE PRODUCERS: *Bischöfliches Priesterseminar, J.J. Christoffel-Erben (Dr. Hermann), Winfried
Berres, R.J. Berres, Geschwister Berres.*

TOWN: **Zeltingen-Rachtig**
GROSSLAGE: Münzlay
EINZELLAGEN (VINEYARDS):
Deutschherrenberg (*v*)               Himmelreich (*v*)                  Sonnenuhr (*e*)
Schlossberg (*g*)
RELIABLE PRODUCERS: *J.J. Prüm*

ANBAUGEBIET: Mosel-Saar-Ruwer                    (Exceptional, *e;* very good, *v;* good, *g.*)

BEREICH: Bernkastel (cont.)

TOWN: **Wehlen**
GROSSLAGE: Münzlay
EINZELLAGEN (VINEYARDS):
Klosterhofgut (*g*)                    Klosterberg (*v*)                    Hofberg (*g*)
Nonnenberg (*v*)                    Sonnenuhr (*e*)                    Abtei (*g*)
RELIABLE PRODUCERS: J.J. Prüm, Peter Prüm (S.A. Prüm-Erben), Zacharias Bergweiler-Prüm, P.J. Prüm-
Erben, Weingut Wwe. Dr. Thanisch

TOWN: **Graach**
GROSSLAGE: Münzlay
EINZELLAGEN (VINEYARDS):
Himmelreich (*e*)                    Domprobst (*v*)                    Abtsberg (*v*)
Josephshöfer (*e*)
RELIABLE PRODUCERS: *von Kesselstatt, Friedrich Wilhelm Gymnasium, Dr. Pauly-Bergweiler.*

TOWN: **Bernkastel-Kues**
GROSSLAGE: Badstube
EINZELLAGEN (VINEYARDS):
Matheisbildchen (*g*)                    Lay (*v*)                    Graben (*e*)
Bratenhöfchen (*g*)                    Doctor (*e*)
RELIABLE PRODUCERS: *St. Johannishof (Dr. Loosen), Lauerburg, Wwe. Dr. Thanisch, Deinhard.*

TOWN: **Lieser**
GROSSLAGE: Beerenlay
EINZELLAGEN (VINEYARDS):
Niederberg-Helden (*g*)                    Sussenberg (*g*)                    Rosenlay (*g*)
Schlossberg (*v*)
RELIABLE PRODUCERS: *von Schorlemer*

ANBAUGEBIET: Mosel-Saar-Ruwer          (Exceptional, *e;* very good, *v;* good, *g.*)

<u>BEREICH: Bernkastel (cont.)</u>

TOWN: **Bernkastel-Kues**
GROSSLAGE: Kurfürstlay
EINZELLAGEN (VINEYARDS):

| | | |
|---|---|---|
| Johannisbrünnchen (g) | Schlossberg (g) | Rosenberg (g) |
| Stephanus-Rosengärtchen (g) | Kardinalsberg (g) | Weissenstein (g) |

TOWN: **Mülheim**
GROSSLAGE: Kurfürstlay
EINZELLAGEN (VINEYARDS):

| | | |
|---|---|---|
| Helenenkloster (e) | Elisenberg (g) | Sonnenlay (e) |
| Amtsgarten (g) | | |

RELIABLE PRODUCERS: *Max Ferdinand Richter.*

TOWN: **Veldenz**
GROSSLAGE: Kurfürstlay
EINZELLAGEN (VINEYARDS):

| | | |
|---|---|---|
| Grafschafter Sonnenberg (g) | Elisenberg (g) | Kirchberg (v) |
| Carlsberg (g) | Mühlberg (g) | |

TOWN: **Brauneberg**
GROSSLAGE: Kurfürstlay
EINZELLAGEN (VINEYARDS):

| | | |
|---|---|---|
| Klostergarten (g) | Mandelgraben (g) | Juffer (e) |
| Juffer-Sonnenuhr (e) | Hasenläufer (g) | Kammer (g) |

RELIABLE PRODUCERS: *von Schorlemer, Weingut Wwe. Dr. Thanisch.*

ANBAUGEBIET: Mosel-Saar-Ruwer                    (Exceptional, *e*; very good, *v*; good, *g*.)

BEREICH: Bernkastel (cont.)

TOWN: **Wintrich**
GROSSLAGE: Kurfürstlay
EINZELLAGEN (VINEYARDS):
Grosser Herrgott (*g*)          Sonnenseite (*g*)          Stefanslay (*g*)
Ohligsberg (*v*)                Geierslay (*v*)
TOWN: **Piesport**
GROSSLAGE: Michelsberg
EINZELLAGEN (VINEYARDS):
Goldtröpfchen (*v*)             Falkenberg (*g*)           Treppchen (*g*)
Günterslay (*g*)                Domherr (*g*)              Gärtchen (*g*)
Kreuzwingert (*g*)              Schubertslay (*g*)         Grafenberg (*g*)
Hofberger (*g*)
RELIABLE PRODUCERS: *von Schorlemer, Vereinigte Hospitien, Bischöfliches Konvikt.*
TOWN: **Neumagen-Dhron**
GROSSLAGE: Michelsberg
EINZELLAGEN (VINEYARDS):
Grosser Hengelberg (*g*)        Grafenberg (*g*)           Roterd (*g*)
Goldtröpfchen (*g*)             Hofberger (*g*)            Häschen (*g*)
Laudamusberg (*g*)              Nusswingert (*g*)          Engelgrube (*v*)
Rosengärtchen (*g*)             Sonnenuhr (*g*)
TOWN: **Trittenheim**
GROSSLAGE: Michelsberg
EINZELLAGEN (VINEYARDS):
Altärchen (*v*)                 Apotheke (*v*)             Felsenkopf (*g*)
Leiterchen (*g*)

ANBAUGEBIET: Mosel-Saar-Ruwer          BEREICH: Saar-Ruwer          (Exceptional, *e*; very good, *v*; good, *g*.)

TOWN: **Avelsbach**
GROSSLAGE: Römerlay
EINZELLAGEN (VINEYARDS):
Hammerstein (*v*)                    Rotlei (*g*)                    Kupp (*v*)
RELIABLE PRODUCERS: *Hohe Domkirche, Staatliches Weinbaudomänen.*

TOWN: **Waldrach**
GROSSLAGE: Römerlay
EINZELLAGEN (VINEYARDS):
Jungfernberg (*g*)          Hubertusberg (*g*)          Sonnenberg (*g*)
Laurentiusberg (*g*)        Ehrenberg (*g*)             Krone (*v*)
Heiligenhäuschen (*g*)      Doktorberg (*g*)            Meisenberg (*g*)
Jesuitengarten (*v*)        Kurfürstenberg (*g*)
RELIABLE PRODUCERS: *Schenck*

TOWN: **Kasel**
GROSSLAGE: Römerlay
EINZELLAGEN (VINEYARDS):
Dominikanerberg (*g*)       Herrenberg (*g*)            Kehrnagel (*v*)
Paulinsberg (*g*)           Nieschen (*v*)              Hitzlay (*v*)
Timpert (*g*)
RELIABLE PRODUCERS: *von Beulwitz, Bischöfliches Konvikt, Bischöfliches Priesterseminar, von Kesselstatt.*

TOWN: **Mertesdorf**
GROSSLAGE: Römerlay
EINZELLAGEN (VINEYARDS):
Mäurchen (*g*)              Johannisberg (*g*)          Felslay (*g*)

AUBAUGEBIET: Mosel-Saar-Ruwer

(Exceptional, e; very good, v; good, g.)

BEREICH: Saar-Ruwer (cont.)

TOWN: **Mertesdorf** (cont.)
GROSSLAGE: Römerlay (cont.)
EINZELLAGEN (VINEYARDS):

| | | |
|---|---|---|
| Herrenberg (v) Ortsteil | Abtsberg (e) Ortsteil | Bruderberg (g) |

RELIABLE PRODUCERS: *von Schubert (Maximin-Grünhaus)*.

TOWN: **Eitelsbach**
GROSSLAGE: Römerlay
EINZELLAGEN (VINEYARDS):

| | | |
|---|---|---|
| Karthäuserhofberg (e) | Marienholz (v) | Burgberg (g) |
| Stirn (g) | Sang (g) | |

RELIABLE PRODUCERS: *Rautenstrauch, Bischöfliches Konvikt*.

TOWN: **Kanzem**
GROSSLAGE: Scharzberg
EINZELLAGEN (VINEYARDS):

| | | |
|---|---|---|
| Altenberg (v) | Schlossberg (g) | Hörecker (g) |
| Sonnenberg (g) | | |

RELIABLE PRODUCERS: *Bischöfliches Priesterseminar*

TOWN: **Oberemmel**
GROSSLAGE: Scharzberg
EINZELLAGEN (VINEYARDS):

| | | |
|---|---|---|
| Karlsberg (g) | Altenberg (g) | Hütte (v) |
| Agritiusberg (g) | Raul (g) | Rosenberg (v) |

RELIABLE PRODUCERS: *Weingut von Kunow (von Hövel), Friedrich Wilhelm Gymnasium, von Kesselstatt*.

ANBAUGEBIET: Mosel-Saar-Ruwer                                    (Exceptional, *e*; very good, *v*; good, *g*.)

BEREICH: Saar-Ruwer (cont.)

TOWN: **Wiltingen**
GROSSLAGE: Scharzberg
EINZELLAGEN (VINEYARDS):

| | |
|---|---|
| Sandberg (g) | Hölle (g) | Kupp (v) |
| Braune Kupp (v) | Gottesfuss (v) | Klosterberg (v) |
| Rosenberg (g) | Braunfels (v) | Schlossberg (g) |
| Schlangengraben (g) | Scharzhofberger (e) Ortsteil | |

RELIABLE PRODUCERS: *Hohe Domkirche, von Kesselstatt, Van Volxem, Egon Müller, Felix Müller, Apollinar Koch.*

TOWN: **Ockfen**
GROSSLAGE: Scharzberg
EINZELLAGEN (VINEYARDS):

| | |
|---|---|
| Herrenberg (v) | Heppenstein (v) | Kupp (g) |
| Bockstein (v) | Zickelgarten (g) | Neuwies (g) |
| Geisberg (v) | | |

RELIABLE PRODUCERS: *Gebert, Fischer, Geltz, Winzerverein Irsch, Weingut Rheinart, Staatliches Wein-baudomänen.*

TOWN: **Ayl**
GROSSLAGE: Scharzberg
EINZELLAGEN (VINEYARDS):

| | |
|---|---|
| Herrenberger (v) | Scheiderberger (g) | Kupp (v) |

RELIABLE PRODUCERS: *The Winzerverein-Ayl, Lauer, Bischöfliches Konvikt.*

ANBAUGEBIET: Mosel-Saar-Ruwer                    (Exceptional, *e;* very good, *v;* good, *g.*)

BEREICH: Saar-Ruwer (cont.)

TOWN: **Saarburg**
GROSSLAGE: Scharzberg
EINZELLAGEN (VINEYARDS):

| | | |
|---|---|---|
| Klosterberg (v) | Fuchs (v) | Stirn (v) |
| Schlossberg (v) | Kupp (g) | Rausch (v) |
| Antoniusbrunnen (g) | Bergschlösschen (g) | Laurentiusberg (g) |

RELIABLE PRODUCERS: *Weingut Rheinart.*

TOWN: **Irsch**
GROSSLAGE: Scharzberg
EINZELLAGEN (VINEYARDS):

| | | |
|---|---|---|
| Hubertusberg (v) | Sonnenberg (g) | Vogelsang (g) |

TOWN: **Serrig**
GROSSLAGE: Scharzberg
EINZELLAGEN (VINEYARDS):

| | | |
|---|---|---|
| Schloss Saarsteiner (g) | Vogelsang (v) | Antoniusberg (g) |
| König Johann Berg (g) | Heiligenborn (v) | Kupp (v) |
| Schloss Saarfelser Schlossberg (g) | Hoeppslei (g) | Würtzberg (g) |
| Herrenberg (g) | | |

RELIABLE PRODUCERS: *Staatliches Weinbaudomänen.*

An **Ortsteil** is confusingly translated as a suburb. In practice, it is the name of a particular estate, which may appear alone on the label without a town name. The right to this prestigious appellation is reserved for those few estates whose fame preceded any laws concerning vineyard names.

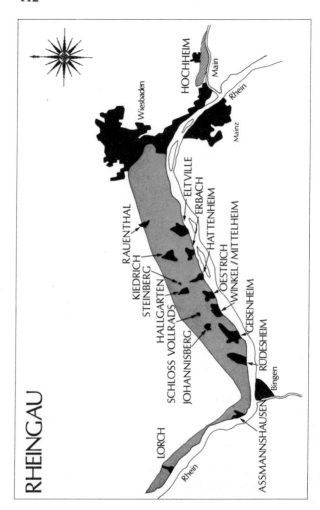

RHEINGAU

## AHR

Red wines are the primary production of the Ahr. Its basic vines are the Pinot Noir (called *Spät-burgunder* in Germany), and a lesser varietal, known as Portugieser. There is only one *Bereich*—Walporzheim/Ahrtal—which contains eleven towns, all of which are entitled to use the *Grosslage* name of Klosterberg.

Since the world has been conditioned to think of white wine when Germany is mentioned, the red wines of the Ahr are almost entirely unrepresented in export markets. The greater part of its production is consumed domestically, although some is exported to neighboring countries that make little wine of their own.

## MITTELRHEIN

This area, which extends from just south of Bonn to near Bingen, is possibly the most strikingly beautiful wine country in the world. The ruins of strategically located castles, which once dominated entire sections of the river, loom high above the towns, while the impossibly steep hillsides are heavily cultivated in Riesling. It is unfortunate that the wines do not live up to their setting. Drunk on the banks of the Rhine, to the imagined strains of Wagnerian tubas, they are often a source of enjoyment, but their ultimate destination remains the province of inexpensive blended table wines, or the processing vat of a cheap *Sekt* (sparkling wine).

## RHEINGAU

The Rheingau is the most prestigious viticultural region in Germany. It is located on the northern bank of the Rhine, extending from Hochheim to just beyond Rüdesheim. From the gentle slopes formed by the foothills of the Taunus Mountains, Riesling wines take on an epic character, dramatized by the famous estates of Prussian counts and princes. The basic Riesling problem is exaggerated here, its unpredictable yield often grossly inadequate in meeting the current demands of the market.

Rheingaus, even in the lower *Prädikat* levels, are rich and full in body: the character of a successful *Beerenauslese* or *Trockenbeerenauslese* may be sufficiently intense to warrant the sharing of a single bottle among a good seven or eight people. (There are, of course, notable variations in style among the quality estates—compare, for example, the archetypal Schloss Johannisberg with the almost Mosel-like delicacy of Schloss Vollrads.)

Rheingau is a relatively small *Anbaugebiet*, and a large quantity of its wine is estate-bottled. Johannisberg is the only *Bereich*, but crammed within it are towns and vineyards that have become the most identifiable wine names of Germany. In fact the extent of the Rheingau's reputation on export markets is strong enough to encourage a particularly exact geographical labeling: genuine association with the area seems to have become an impressive stimulus to both quality and local pride.

There are some growers here who own prime, but limited areas of land. Under such circumstances, they do better to sell their production for vinification and bottling to a regional cooperative cellar, which is partly subsidized by the German government. Known as *Winzergenossenschäfte,* such institutions will be clearly indicated in the place of the producer on the label. (The term *Winzerverein* means entirely the same thing, but is normally applied to Mosel cooperatives.)

The State maintains a wine school on the Rheingau at Kloster Eberbach, an impeccably preserved monastic complex begun in the twelfth century. Also headquartered here is the *Staatsweingüter,* wine authority for the area, and producer of wines from Erbach, Rauenthal, Rüdesheim, and the great Steinberg vineyard (close to Kloster Eberbach itself). Not only are these wines excellent in their own right, but the revenue produced by their sales is laudably applied to the general improvement of the German wine industry.

(Exceptional, *e*; very good, *v*; good, *g*.)

ANBAUGEBIET: Rheingau

BEREICH: Johannisberg

TOWN: **Assmannshausen/Aulhausen** (red wine)
GROSSLAGE: Steil
EINZELLAGEN (VINEYARDS):

Frankenthal (g)                Höllenberg (g)            Hintekirch (g)
Berg Kaisersteinfels (g)
RELIABLE PRODUCERS: *Staatsweingüter.*

TOWN: **Rüdesheim**
GROSSLAGE: Burweg
EINZELLAGEN (VINEYARDS):

Berg Roseneck (v)              Berg Rottland (v)         Bishofsberg (v)
Berg Schlossberg (v)           Drachenstein (g)          Kirchenpfad (g)
Klosterberg (g)                Magdalenendreuz (g)       Klosterlay (g)
Rosengarten (g)
RELIABLE PRODUCERS: *von Ritter zu Groenestyn, Staatsweingüter.*

TOWN: **Geisenheim**
GROSSLAGE: Burweg
EINZELLAGEN (VINEYARDS):

Rothenberg (v)                 Kläuserweg (g)            Fuchsberg (g)
Kilzberg (g)                   Mäuerchen (g)             Mönchspfad (g)
Schlossgarten (g)              Klaus (v)
RELIABLE PRODUCERS: *Frieherr von Zwierlein Erben, Staatliches Lehr-und Forschungsanstalt für Wein- Obst-und Gartenbau.*

ANBAUGEBIET: Rheingau

(Exceptional, *e*; very good, *v*; good, *g*.)

BEREICH: Johannisberg (cont.)

TOWN: **Johannisberg**
GROSSLAGE: Erntebringer
EINZELLAGEN (VINEYARDS):
Schwarzenstein (*g*)                 Vogelsang (*g*)          Hölle (*g*)
Hansenberg (*g*)                     Goldatzel (*g*)          Klaus (*v*)
Schloss Johannisberg (*e*)           Mittelhölle (*g*)
  Ortsteil
RELIABLE PRODUCERS: *Landgräflich Hessische Weingut, Fürst von Metternich.*
TOWN: **Winkel**
GROSSLAGE: Honigberg
EINZELLAGEN (VINEYARDS):
Gutenberg (*g*)                      Dachsberg (*g*)          Schlossberg (*g*)
Jesuitengarten (*v*)                 Hasensprung (*g*)        Klaus (*v*)
Schloss Vollrads (*e*) Ortsteil      Bienengarten (*g*)
RELIABLE PRODUCERS: *von Brentano, Graf Matuschka Greiffenclau'sches.*
TOWN: **Mittelheim**
GROSSLAGE: Honigberg
EINZELLAGEN (VINEYARDS):
St. Nikolaus (*g*)                   Edelmann (*g*)           Goldberg (*g*)
TOWN: **Oestrich**
GROSSLAGE: Gottesthal
EINZELLAGEN (VINEYARDS):
Klosterberg (*g*)                    Lenchen (*g*)            Doosberg (*v*)
Schloss Rheinhartshausen (*e*)
  Ortsteil
RELIABLE PRODUCERS: *Prinz von Preussen.*

(Exceptional, *e*; very good, *v*; good, *g*.)

ANBAUGEBIET: Rheingau

BEREICH: Johannisberg (cont.)

TOWN: **Hattenheim**
GROSSLAGE: Deutelsberg
EINZELLAGEN (VINEYARDS):
Wisselbrunnen (*v*)                    Nussbrunnen (*g*)          Mannberg (*e*)
Heiligenberg (*g*)                     Schützenhaus (*g*)         Hassel (*g*)
Steinberger (*e*)/Ortsteil            Pfaffenberg (*v*)          Engelmannsberg (*v*)
RELIABLE PRODUCERS: *Langwerth von Simmern, Staatsweingüter.*

TOWN: **Hallgarten**
GROSSLAGE: Mehrhölzchen
EINZELLAGEN (VINEYARDS):
Schönhell (*v*)                        Würzgarten (*g*)           Jungfer (*v*)
Hendelberg (*v*)
RELIABLE PRODUCERS: *Fürst von Löwenstein-Wertheim-Rosenberg'sches Weingut.*

TOWN: **Erbach**
GROSSLAGE: Mehrhölzchen
EINZELLAGEN (VINEYARDS):
Marcobrunn (*e*)                       Schlossberg (*g*)          Siegelsberg (*v*)
Honigberg (*g*)                        Michelmark (*v*)           Hohenrain (*v*)
Steinmorgen (*v*)                      Reinhell (*v*)
RELIABLE PRODUCERS: *Winzergenossenschaft, Staatsweingüter, Weingut Erbacherhof (Wagner-Weritz), Kohlhass, von Oettinger.*

TOWN: **Kiedrich**
GROSSLAGE: Heiligenstock
EINZELLAGEN (VINEYARDS):
Klosterberg (*g*)                      Gräfenberg (*v*)           Wasseros (*v*)

ANBAUGEBIET: Rheingau

BEREICH: Johannisberg (cont.)

(Exceptional, *e*; very good, *v*; good, *g*.)

TOWN: **Kiedrich** (cont.)
GROSSLAGE: Heiligenstock (cont.)
EINZELLAGEN (VINEYARDS):
Sandgrub (*v*)
RELIABLE PRODUCERS: *Dr. Weil, Staatsweingüter.*

TOWN: **Eltville**
GROSSLAGE: Heiligenstock
EINZELLAGEN (VINEYARDS):
Taubenberg (*v*)                    Langenstück (*v*)          Sonnenberg (*e*)
Rheinberg (*g*)                     Sandgrub (*g*)
RELIABLE PRODUCERS: *Schloss Eltz (Gräflich Eltz'sche Gutsverwaltung).*

TOWN: **Rauenthal**
GROSSLAGE: Steinmächer
EINZELLAGEN (VINEYARDS):
Baiken (*e*)                        Gehrn (*v*)                Wülfen (*v*)
Rothenberg (*v*)                    Langenstück (*g*)          Nonnenberg (*g*)
RELIABLE PRODUCERS: *Staatsweingüter, von Simmern.*

TOWN: **Hochheim**
GROSSLAGE: Daubhaus
EINZELLAGEN (VINEYARDS):
Königin Victoriaberg (*v*)          Hofmeister (*g*)           Stielweg (*v*)
Sommergeil (*g*)                    Domdechaney (*v*)          Hölle (*v*)
Kirchenstück (*v*)                  Reichesthal (*g*)          Berg (*g*)
Herrnberg (*g*)                     Stein (*v*)
RELIABLE PRODUCERS: *Aschrott, von Schönborn, Prinz von Preussen, Staatsweingüter.*

## NAHE

The most important wines of the River Nahe (which joins the Rhine just west of Bingen) are made at Schlossböckelheim and, further north, in the town of Bad Kreuznach. They possess flavors that are entirely their own, full-bodied with a strong hint of spice, characteristics that are mostly absent in other Nahe wines. Paul Anheuser and the state-owned vineyards at Schlossböckelheim are among the better producers, while grape varieties are roughly divided into equal allotments of Riesling, Sylvaner, and Müller-Thurgau.

## RHEINHESSEN

The almost global fame of the Rheinhessen is largely attributable to its appearance as the most common *Anbaugebiet* of *Liebfraumilch*. Although a boon for the bulk wine business of the entire region, the association has detracted significantly from the success of serious growers. If we remove the massive quantities of regional wines from the area's total export figures, it is immediately apparent that the real Rheinhessens do not share in the popularity of their neighbors to the north and west.

The products of lesser grapes can often be impressive in the cellars of a good vintner, while thoroughbred Rieslings take on a marked heaviness in good years, quite unlike the more complex wines of the Rheingau. In poor years, the Rheinhessen will often benefit from its southerly latitude and warmer growing season.

(Exceptional, *e;* very good, *v;* good, *g.*)

ANBAUGEBIET: Rheinhessen      BEREICH: Nierstein

TOWN: **Nierstein**
GROSSLAGE: Spiegelberg
EINZELLAGEN (VINEYARDS):

| | | |
|---|---|---|
| Rosenberg (g) | Klostergarten (g) | Findling (g) |
| Kirchplatte (g) | Schloss Hohenrechen (g) | Ebersberg (g) |
| Bildstock (g) | Brückchen (g) | Paterberg (v) |
| Hölle (g) | | |

RELIABLE PRODUCERS: *Emil Förster, von Heil zu Herrnsheim, Louis Guntrum, Wwe. Franz Karl Schmitt, Rheinhold Senfter, George Albrecht Schneider.*

TOWN: **Nierstein**
GROSSLAGE: Rehbach
EINZELLAGEN (VINEYARDS):

| | | |
|---|---|---|
| Pettenthal (v) | Brudersberg (g) | Hipping (v) |
| Goldene Luft (g) | | |

TOWN: **Nierstein**
GROSSLAGE: Auflangen
EINZELLAGEN (VINEYARDS):

| | | |
|---|---|---|
| Kranzberg (g) | Zehnmorgen (g) | Bergkirche (g) |
| Heiligenbaum (g) | Glück (g) | Ölberg (v) |
| Schloss Schwabsburg (g) | Orbel (v) | |

TOWN: **Oppenheim**
GROSSLAGE: Güldenmorgen
EINZELLAGEN (VINEYARDS):

| | | |
|---|---|---|
| Zuckerberg (g) | Daubhaus (g) | Herrenberg (g) |
| Sackträger (v) | Schützenhütte (g) | Kreuz (v) |

**ANBAUGEBIET: Rheinhessen**    <u>BEREICH: Nierstein (cont.)</u>    (Exceptional, *e;* very good, *v;* good, *g.*)

**TOWN: Oppenheim** (cont.)
GROSSLAGE: Güldenmorgen (cont.)
EINZELLAGEN (VINEYARDS):
Gutleuthaus (*g*)
RELIABLE PRODUCERS: *Franz Josef Gallois, Karl Koch, F.J. Senfter, Ernst Jungkenn, Weingut der Stadt Oppenheim, Friedrich Baumann.*

**TOWN: Dienheim**
GROSSLAGE: Güldenmorgen
EINZELLAGEN (VINEYARDS):

| | | |
|---|---|---|
| Falkenberg (*g*) | Herrenberg (*g*) | Kreuz (*v*) |
| Siliusbrunnen (*v*) | Höhlchen (*g*) | Tafelstein (*g*) |

**TOWN: Oppenheim**
GROSSLAGE: Krötenbrunnen
EINZELLAGEN (VINEYARDS):

| | | |
|---|---|---|
| Schlossberg (*g*) | Schloss (*v*) | Paterhof (*g*) |
| Herrengarten (*g*) | | |

**TOWN: Dienheim**
GROSSLAGE: Krötenbrunnen
EINZELLAGEN (VINEYARDS):

| | | |
|---|---|---|
| Herrengarten (*g*) | Paterhof (*g*) | Schloss (*v*) |

<u>BEREICH: Wonnegau</u>

**TOWN: Worms**
GROSSLAGE: Liebfrauenmorgen
EINZELLAGEN (VINEYARDS):

| | | |
|---|---|---|
| St. Cyriakusstift (*g*) | Remeyerhof (*g*) | Lerchelsberg (*g*) |

ANBAUGEBIET: Rheinhessen

(Exceptional, *e*; very good, *v*; good, *g*.)

BEREICH: Wonnegau (cont.)

TOWN: **Worms** (cont.)
GROSSLAGE: Liebfrauenmorgen (cont.)
EINZELLAGEN (VINEYARDS):

St. Georgenberg (*g*)          Hochberg (*g*)          Sankt Annaberg (*g*)
Liebfrauenstift-Kirchenstück    Römersteg (*g*)         Nonnenwingert (*g*)
(*v*)

Am Heiligen Häuschen (*g*)     Goldberg (*g*)          Burgweg (*g*)
Kreuzblick (*g*)               Affenberg (*g*)         Schneckenberg (*g*)
Kapellenstück (*g*)            Klausenberg (*g*)       Goldpfad (*g*)
Bildstock (*g*)                Rheinberg (*g*)
RELIABLE PRODUCERS: *Valckenberg, Langenbach.*

### HESSISCHE BERGSTRASSE

This is the smallest of the *Anbaugebiete*, its products rarely appearing on the export market. Poor shipping properties are largely attributable to characteristically low acid levels, and have generally restricted the wines to domestic distribution.

### RHEINPFALZ

The Rheinpfalz (known also as the Palatinate) is the most southerly of the quality *Anbaugebiete*. Relatively good weather has encouraged the planting of a broad range of grapes, extending even to the Portugieser, and occasionally the Spätburgunder (Pinot Noir), for reds and rosés.

The whites, of course, are the most important, originating in the Gewürztraminer, Traminer, Rülander, and Morio-Muscat, together with the more common Sylvaner, Müller-Thurgau, and Riesling. A warm growing season produces grapes that are richer in natural sugar—and higher in potential alcohol.

Second largest of Germany's wine making regions, the vineyards of the Rheinpfalz occupy a good 50,000 acres parallel and to the west of the Rhine's principal course. With the exception of the famous estates of the region between Bad Dürkheim and Deidesheim, the wines at best are the stuff of regional bottlings.

(Exceptional, *e*; very good, *v*; good, *g*.)

ANBAUGEBIET: Rheinpfalz
BEREICH: Mittelhaardt Deutsche Weinstrasse

TOWN: **Bad Dürkheim**
GROSSLAGE: Hochmess
EINZELLAGEN (VINEYARDS): Michelsberg (*v*)  Spielberg (*g*)  Hochbenn (*g*)
Rittergarten (*g*)
RELIABLE PRODUCERS: *Karl Schaefer.*
TOWN: **Bad Dürkheim**
GROSSLAGE: Schenkenböhl
EINZELLAGEN (VINEYARDS): Fuchsmantel (*g*)  Fronhof (*g*)
Abtsfronhof (*g*)
TOWN: **Wachenheim**
GROSSLAGE: Schenkenböhl
EINZELLAGEN (VINEYARDS): Fuchsmantel (*v*)  Odinstal (*g*)
Königswingert (*g*)  Schlossberg (*g*)
Mandelgarten (*g*)
TOWN: **Wachenheim**
GROSSLAGE: Schnepfenflug an der Weinstrasse
EINZELLAGEN (VINEYARDS): Luginsland (*v*)
Bischofsgarten (*g*)
RELIABLE PRODUCERS: *Bürklin-Wolf.*
TOWN: **Forst**
GROSSLAGE: Schnepfenflug an der Weinstrasse
EINZELLAGEN (VINEYARDS): Süsskopf (*g*)  Stift (*g*)
Bischofsgarten (*g*)

(Exceptional, *e*; very good, *v*; good, *g*.)

ANBAUGEBIET: Rheinpfalz
    BEREICH: Mittlehaardt Deutsche Weinstrasse (cont.)

TOWN: **Deidesheim**
GROSSLAGE: Schnepfenflug an der Weinstrasse
EINZELLAGEN (VINEYARDS):
Letten (*g*)

TOWN: **Wachenheim**
GROSSLAGE: Mariengarten
EINZELLAGEN (VINEYARDS):

| | | |
|---|---|---|
| Böhlig (*g*) | Belz (*g*) | Rechbächel (*v*) |
| Goldbächel (*g*) | Gerümpel (*e*) | Altenburg (*v*) |

TOWN: **Forst**
GROSSLAGE: Mariengarten
EINZELLAGEN (VINEYARDS):

| | | |
|---|---|---|
| Musenhang (*g*) | Pechstein (*g*) | Ungeheuer (*v*) |
| Jesuitengarten (*v*) | Kirchenstück (*e*) | Elster (*g*) |
| Freundstück (*v*) | | |

RELIABLE PRODUCERS: *Bassermann-Jordan.*

TOWN: **Deidesheim**
GROSSLAGE: Mariengarten
EINZELLAGEN (VINEYARDS):

| | | |
|---|---|---|
| Herrgottsacker (*e*) | Mäushöhle (*v*) | Kieselberg (*g*) |
| Hohenmorgen (*g*) | Grainhübel (*e*) | Kalkofen (*g*) |
| Paradiesgarten (*g*) | Langenmorgen (*g*) | Leinhöhle (*v*) |
| Nonnenstück (*g*) | | |

(Hofstück is the other possible Grosslage for Deidesheim.)

## BADEN

Surrounding Bodensee near the Swiss border, the *Anbaugebiet* of Baden is planted mostly in white wine grapes, with a strong tendency toward Riesling and Morio-Muscat. Although fragrant and easy to drink in their youth, the wines of the area have found little place in foreign markets.

## WÜRTTEMBERG

The red wine production of Württemberg closely rivals its white, while both seem to end up in the carafes of regional cafés in nearby Karlsruhe, Heidelberg, Stuttgart, and other local towns. The style here is hearty, and best enjoyed when still young. Also known as "wines of the Neckar" (from the River Neckar, which will join the Rhine at Mannheim), they will occasionally show up on shippers' lists, but no single town or vineyard stands out.

## FRANKEN

Franconia's central attraction is the city of Würzburg, which is also home to Stein and Leiste, the area's principal vineyards. The basic grape is the Sylvaner, so often frowned upon in other parts of Germany as a vine of abundance rather than quality. Its well-balanced dry whites are relatively expensive, often resembling the good white Burgundies (in the real sense), not only in price, but also in quality and application.

GERMAN VINTAGES
*(as of 1977)*

1976    Great *Prädikat* wines produced in the Rheingau and Saar-Ruwer: *Q.b.A.* and *Kabinett* yield was low. Other areas somewhat too high in residual sugar, departing from the traditional balance.

1975    The Mosel led the way in quality. That vital acid-sugar balance was perfect in a high yield of potentially long-lived wines. The other areas were also very good, but many were sold at unreasonably high prices on the strength of the Mosel vintage.

1974    Essentially a vintage of *Q.b.A.* and *Tafelwein* quality. The few *Prädikat* wines were mostly *Kabinett*. Considerable crop loss caused by late-season rain. Reasonably sound, but low in fruit.

1973    A gigantic, good harvest. Almost all areas produced wines of above average quality. Decent prices due to abundance.

1972    Very soft, and already fading rapidly. Only the choicest vineyards remain of interest.

1971    What was proclaimed "vintage of the century" has yet to be disappointing. Most have been drunk too young, and supplies have dwindled: many are only just beginning to show their nobility.

Wines made prior to 1971 can still be very good, especially if the *Prädikat* is *Auslese* or above. It remains a safe practice to buy the sweeter *Prädikats* in any vintage because they are, by definition, the production of an exceptional year. The following are highly recommended: 1970, 1967, 1964, 1959, 1957, 1953, 1949, and 1943.

# Appendix B
# The Wines of France

THE French have seemingly infused their dining habits with the principles of national pride. Whether it be the *bouillabaisse* of Marseilles with the chilled wines of Cassis, or the Charolais beef from Burgundy accompanied by a rich Chambertin, there is an almost divine sense of purpose in the traditional partnerships of food and wine.

To compare the wines of a particular area with the peculiarities of local attitudes is the recurring weakness of the visiting oenophile. The lofty elegance of the Loires, the rural simplicity of the wines of the South, and the rigid austerity of the serious Médocs can all be interpreted as statements of regional feeling. An apple farmer in the North will rarely devote himself to the gastronomic delights of red Burgundy: the inspiration of country cooking is the singular province of home.

# FRANCE

It may also be that the French wine maker is more in tune with his region's heritage. His techniques have been refined by the innovations of modern science, but he continues to feel the profound influence of the land. In the final analysis, change comes to him slowly, and his product reflects the best efforts of prior generations.

The standards of French wine are set by a government agency, known as the *Institut Nationale des Appellations d'Origine des Vins et Eaux-de-Vie.* Quality control in France relies on the universal assumption that certain regions excel in the cultivation of particular grape varieties. By so limiting the production of an area, and at the same time restricting the yield of individual vineyards, it is possible to guarantee certain minimum standards of quality. Other considerations extend to the nature of agricultural practice and the actual process of vinification, both of which are subject to regional variation. When the vintner satisfies the authorities in all respects, he is allowed the privilege of selling his wine with an official certificate of *Appellation.* That *Appellation Contrôlée* then becomes the consumer's guarantee that the wine is actually what it claims to be. It is a statement that is more or less a prerequisite for wines of export quality, while products with lesser authorizations— *Appellations d'Origine Simple* and *Vins Délimités de Qualité Supérieure (V.D.Q.S.,* or "delimited wines of superior quality")—are only shipped under the most doubtful conditions.

In the category of greatness, however, the certificate of *Appellation* is somewhat redundant. It is in-

*1976* [1]

MONOPOLE

# LA BARRIQE D'OR [2]

## BORDEAUX [3]

APPELLATION BORDEAUX CONTROLEE [4]

**P. Lequinche** [5]

NEGOCIANT A BORDEAUX [6]

Mis en Bouteille à Bordeaux [7]

---

VIN DE BOURGOGNE [1]

MISE AU DOMAINE [2]

1976 [3]

# SAINT~VERAN [4]

Appellation St-Véran Contrôlée [5]

# Clos Victor [6]

*Jean Arris, Viticulteur à Torpoint* [7]

## THE FRENCH WINE LABEL

*The Regional Wine*
The wine may be called by its *monopole* (brand name) or by a region of geographical origin sufficiently broad to allow the shipper many blending opportunities.

1. The vintage.
2. Either the *monopole* or the area of origin.
3. An essentially generic term that occasionally appears to aid consumer identification.
4. The *Appellation Contrôlée* statement, naming the place of origin.
5. The shipper.
6. The *négociant*: one who deals in the buying and selling of wine.
7. This is an almost meaningless statement: "Bottled (somewhere) in Bordeaux". The shipper hopes to confuse the unwary buyer who might associate the phrase with the conventional statement of estate bottling (No. 2 below).

*The Estate Wine*
The wine of a single property within an *Appellation*.

1. The viticultural region of origin.
2. The guarantee of estate bottling. This particular phrase is common in Burgundy and the Rhône: in Bordeaux, *Mis en Bouteille au Château* is a precise equivalent.
3. The vintage.
4. The specific authorized place name.
5. The *Appellation* statement.
6. The name of the estate.
7. It is common to state the name and address of the proprietor: the ultimate responsibility for the product will always be assumed by some named person or entity.

creasingly apparent that technically sound wines can be produced quickly and efficiently to satisfy the needs of a bulk marketing system, while remaining perfectly entitled to *Appellation Contrôlée* status. Greatness, on the other hand, is clearly above the law, and minimum standards are of little value to the conscientious wine maker.

We should therefore familiarize ourselves with the essential differences between the label of an estate-bottled wine and that of a regional product (which is usually the blended wine of a commune or large group of vintners). While an estate-bottling is not necessarily better, it continues to represent that intensely personal relationship between the wine maker and the object of his creation. The work of a poorly-defined group is all too frequently the product of nothing more than the observation of those minimum standards.

## BURGUNDY

Burgundy's reputation stems from its production of impressively sturdy, dry red and white wines. It is a rural area of France and were it not on the main route from Paris to the South, there would be little (except wine) to justify a visit. Dijon, to the North, and Mâcon and Lyon in the nearby southern sections are busy urban centers, but the feel of country agriculture is immediately apparent wherever the vines grow.

The laws of *Appellation* specify five Burgundy areas: Chablis, Chalonnais, Mâconnais, Beaujolais, and the Côte d'Or (subdivided into the Côte de Nuits and Côte de Beaune). The lowest *Appellation* a wine from these areas may hold is Bourgogne Grand Ordinaire, meaning that the wine is of 9% alcohol and was made from the legal Burgundy grapes (grapes will be discussed later in this chapter). Due to its low alcohol content and consequent instability, the wine is rarely shipped beyond its region of origin. This is the staple offering of local cafés where its inexpensive and youthful character is especially appropriate.

Above Bourgogne Grand Ordinaire come two *Appellations*, Bourgogne Aligoté and Bourgogne Passetoutgrains. The former, which is strictly a white wine, is occasionally deficient in acid and inclined to be overly soft. When carefully made, however, it can often bear a delightful resemblance to its white Chardonnay neighbors. The less popular Passetoutgrains is a blend of one third Gamay plus Pinot varieties. In their excellent work on

# BURGUNDY

Burgundy, Arlott and Fielden have cautioned that Passetoutgrains, however low the price, is not a wine to be gulped when young: rather, it takes several years in the bottle before the Pinot character can come through to make for pleasant drinking.

The *Appellation Contrôlée* of Bourgogne is slightly higher in quality. Although the simplicity of the name often fails to catch the consumer's eye, many of these are surprisingly good. The label will bear some reference to a shipper or grower, and we occasionally find ourselves drinking a wine that might have been made to be sold under a far more prestigious name. (The laws that limit the production of *Appellation Controlee* wines cause this to occur under certain stated conditions, and such wines are usually an exceptional value.) On the other hand, wine made solely for Bourgogne purposes is subjected to reasonably high standards and, due to lack of popularity, there is almost no commercial reason for tampering. The odd purchase of a sample bottle can never be too disappointing.

Quality improves further with the mentioning of place names on the label. Although very broad terms may be used, the description becomes sharply narrower as standards increase. Furthermore, as the vintner becomes more specific in stating the place of origin, so the legal controls with regard to vinification become proportionately rigid. For example, a vintner who holds land in the town of Chassagne-Montrachet in the Côte de Beaune can always submit his wine under the *Appellation* of Bourgogne. If, however, the wine was made for a more prestigious *Appellation*, he must arrange to prove to the authorities that the production limits for, say, Chassagne-Montrachet were not exceeded, and that his methods of vinification were in compliance with the minimum standards. The difference in revenue makes it well worth his trouble. On the other hand, he might say that his wine is of an even higher quality, and that, in the event of a good vintage, his production now warrants the name of the vineyard (in this case, the Abbaye de Morgeot). It is only at the end of each harvest that the vintner decides what *Appellations* his wines are likely to achieve. Should a wine fail at the level of his choice, he has no declassification options, and his production is distilled or made into vinegar.

The label is an indicator of a wine's status in the Burgundy hierarchy. The best are actually the simplest. Those that bear the name of a vineyard (Musigny, Corton, etc.) with no reference to a town are described as *Grands Crus*. *Premier Cru* vineyards must state the town name, while the name of the vineyard is still permissible in letters of the same size. For lesser wines, the vineyard name may only appear in smaller print. In actual commercial practice, wines that are not of *Premier Cru* status are usually sold as village wines. (The former village habit of annexing the name of a well-known vineyard can be confusing, but is normally made clear by the use of a hyphen between the two names: so a Chambolle-Musigny is strictly a village wine and not a Musigny.)

There are two white wine grapes of importance in the Burgundy area, the Chardonnay and the Aligoté, while the Pinot Noir, Pinot Gris, Pinot

Liebault, and Gamay are all grown for the production of reds. The actual combinations that may legally be used will vary from one area to another. In general, the bulk of the Gamay occurs in Beaujolais and cannot be included in any of the *Bourgogne Appellations*, with the exception of the *Grand Cru* towns of Beaujolais itself. Because Aligoté is financially unrewarding, Chardonnay has become a preferable choice when the area is conducive to its success.

*Chablis*

Geographically, Chablis is disconnected from Burgundy proper, situated to the northwest between the towns of Auxerre and Tonnerre. Its wines, made from the Chardonnay, are nevertheless closely related. The term Chablis has become synonymous with white wine in general in many countries outside France: in the United States especially, it is used to sell jug wines that are often slightly sweet. This is a radical departure from the superlative, bone-dry whites that come in such sparing quantities from Chablis itself. But the English-speaking world is not the only culprit in the game of misrepresentation. A look at the production figures for a high-yield vintage conflicts dramatically with the sheer volume of Chablis—all bottled in France—that is universally available in retail situations.

Honest Chablis is marvelous but certainly never a bargain; and even the impostors will cost nearly as much as the genuine article. Be wary of those strangely-priced, overly-fancy labels: if you do not know the producer, and savings are the main consideration, look for something smaller at a real price. Muscadet, Bourgogne Blanc, or Petit-Chablis are often sound alternatives.

BURGUNDY: **Chablis**

(Exceptional, *e*; very good, *v*; good, *g*.)

Beauroy (*v*)
Beugnon (*v*)
Blanchots (*e*)
Bougros (*e*)
Buttereaux (*v*)
Chapelot (*v*)
Chatain (*v*)
Côte de Fontenay (*v*)
Côte de Lèchet (*v*)
Côte de Vaillon (*v*)

Les Forêts (*v*)
Fourchaume (*v*)
Grenouilles (*e*)
Les Clos (*e*)
Les Cys (*v*)
Les Preuses (*e*)
Mélinots (*v*)
Mont de Milieu (*v*)
Montée de Tonnerre (*v*)
Montmain (*v*)

Pied d'Aloup (*v*)
Séchet (*v*)
Troesmes (*v*)
Vaillon (*v*)
Valmur (*e*)
Vosgros (*v*)
Vaucoupin (*v*)
Vaudésir (*e*)
Vaulorent (*v*)
Vaupulent (*v*)

Other possible *Appellations:*
**Chablis Premier Cru:** a blend of more than one of the Premier Crus (*v*) above.
**Chablis** and **Petit-Chablis:** regional *Appellations*. The production of good, but not exceptional blends.

RELIABLE PRODUCERS: *Henri LaRoche, J. Billaud-Simon, Reynier (Regnard), Domaine de la Maladière.* Apart from the above, we hesitate to make liberal recommendations. It is generally true that shippers' wines from Chablis will fluctuate in quality from vintage to vintage. Estate-bottled wines are generally reliable.

*The Côte de Nuits*

Here we find red Burgundy at its absolute finest. Every available acre of land is rich in Pinot Noir and home to some of the greatest of the Burgundy vineyards: La Tache, Romanée-Conti, Richebourg, Clos de Vougeot, Chambertin—the list is seemingly endless. A grower in the Côte de Nuits has only to bring his vines to fruition in order to luxuriate in a market where demand greatly exceeds supply.

The narrow strip that stretches northwards toward Dijon is now under maximum cultivation, its gentle slopes offering perfect properties of drainage and exposure to the heat of the sun. The vines are often old, twisted, and gnarled, their roots sunk deep into the rich, red earth for water and nourishment.

Our reference lists deal only with the *Premier Cru* and *Grand Cru* vineyards. Lesser wines are not likely to be marketed in the United States under a vineyard name, but blended together and sold instead as village wine. Under the auspices of a reliable shipper, the results can be excellent, but for a few pennies more it is often worthwhile to invest in one of the less well-known *Premiers Crus*.

(Exceptional, *e*; very good, *v*; good, *g*.)

BURGUNDY: The Côte de Nuits

**TOWN: Fixin**

| | | |
|---|---|---|
| les Arvelets (*v*) | Clos du Chapitre (*v*) | les Meix Bas (*v*) |
| Au Cheusots (*v*) | les Hervelets (*v*) | la Perrière (*v*) |

**TOWN: Gevrey-Chambertin**

| | | |
|---|---|---|
| Bel Air (*v*) | Combottes (*v*) | Mazys-Chambertin (*e*) |
| Chambertin (*e*) | les Corbeaux (*v*) | Mazoyères-Chambertin (*e*) |
| Chambertin Clos de Bèze (*e*) | Etournelles (*v*) | la Petite Chapelle ou Champitonnois (*v*) |
| les Champeaux (*v*) | le Fonteny (*v*) | le Poissenot (*v*) |
| Champonnets (*v*) | Gazetiers (*v*) | Ruchottes du Bas (*e*) |
| Chapelle-Chambertin (*e*) | Gemeaux (*v*) | Ruchottes du Dessus (*e*) |
| aux Charmes (*e*) | les Goulots (*v*) | Saint-Jacques (*v*) |
| Charmes-Chambertin (*e*) | Griotte-Chambertin (*e*) | Véroilles (*v*) |
| Cherbaudes (*v*) | Latricières-Chambertin (*e*) | |
| Clos Prieur (*v*) | Lavaux (*v*) | |
| Combe aux Moines (*v*) | Mazys Bas (*e*) | |

**TOWN: Morey-Saint-Denis**

| | | |
|---|---|---|
| les Blanchards (*v*) | Clos Bussière (*v*) | les Gruanchers (*v*) |
| les Bonnes Mares (*e*) | Clos des Ormes (*v*) | les Herbuottes (*v*) |
| Calouère (*v*) | Clos de la Roche (*e*) | Maison Brulée (*e*) |
| les Chabiots (*e*) | Clos Saint-Denis (*e*) | Meix Rentiers (*v*) |
| les Chaffots (*v*) | Clos Sorbés (*v*) | les Millandes (*v*) |
| aux Charmes (*v*) | Clos de Tart (*e*) | les Mochamps (*e*) |
| les Charrières (*v*) | Façonnières (*v*) | Monts Luisants (*e*) |
| les Chénevery (*v*) | les Frémières (*e*) | la Riotte (*v*) |
| aux Chezaux (*v*) | les Froichots (*e*) | les Ruchots (*v*) |
| Clos Baulet (*v*) | les Genevrières (*e*) | les Sorbés (*v*) |

(Exceptional, *e*; very good, *v*; good, *g*.)

les Hauts Doix (*v*)
les Lavrottes (*v*)
les Musigny (*e*)
les Noirots (*v*)
les Petits Musigny (*e*)
les Plantes (*v*)
les Sentiers (*v*)

les Poulaillières (*e*)
les Rouges du Bas (*e*)
les Rouges des Dessus (*e*)
les Treux (*e*)
Vigne Blanche ou Clos
    Blanc de Vougeot (*v*)

Romanée-Conti (*e*)
Romanée Saint-Vivant (*v*)
les Suchots (*v*)
la Tâche (*e*)
Verroilles ou Richebourg (*v*)

les Corvées Paget (*v*)
les Didiers (*v*)
aux Perdrix (*v*)

BURGUNDY: The Côte de Nuits
TOWN: **Chambolle-Musigny**
les Amoureuses (*v*)
les Barottes (*v*)
les Bonnes-Mares (*e*)
les Borniques (*v*)
les Carrières (*v*)
les Charmes (*v*)
les Châtelots (*v*)

les Cras (*v*)
Derrière Grange (*v*)
les Fousselottes (*v*)
les Fuées (*v*)
les Grands Murs (*v*)
les Groseilles (*v*)
les Gruenchers (*v*)

TOWN: **Vougeot** (includes **Flagey-Echezeaux**)
les Beaumonts Bas (*v*)
les Beaumonts Hauts (*v*)
les Cartiers de Nuits (*e*)
les Champs Traversins (*e*)
Clos Saint-Denis (*e*)
Clos de Vougeot (*e*)
les Cras (*v*)

les Cruots ou Vignes
    Blanches (*e*)
Echezeaux du Dessus (*e*)
les Grands Echezeaux (*e*)
les Loachausses (*e*)
en Orveaux (*e*)
les Petits Vougeots (*e*)

TOWN: **Vosne-Romanée**
aux Bas de Combe (*v*)
Clos de Réas (*v*)
la Croix Rameau (*v*)
au Dessus de Malconsorts (*v*)
Gros Parantoux (*v*)

aux Malconsorts (*v*)
les Petits Monts (*v*)
les Reignots (*v*)
les Richebourg (*e*)
Romanée (*e*)

TOWN: **Prémeaux** (*Appellation* **Nuits St. Georges**)
les Argillières (*v*)
Clos Arlots (*v*)
le Clos des Corvées (*v*)

le Clos des Forêts (*v*)
Clos de la Maréchale (*v*)
les Clos Saint-Marc (*v*)

(Exceptional, *e*; very good, *v*; good, *g*.)

BURGUNDY: The Côte de Nuits
TOWN: **Nuits Saint-Georges**

aux Boudots (*v*)
aux Bousselots (*v*)
les Cailles (*v*)
les Chaboeufs (*v*)
aux Chaignots (*v*)
Chaine Carteau (*v*)
aux Cras (*v*)
aux Crots (*v*)

aux Damodes (*v*)
aux Murgers (*v*)
la Perrière (*v*)
les Porrets (*v*)
les Poulettes (*v*)
les Procès (*v*)
les Pruliers (*v*)
le Richemone (*v*)

Roncière (*v*)
Rue de Chaux (*v*)
les Saint-Georges (*v*)
aux Thorey (*v*)
les Vaucrains (*v*)
aux Vignes Rondes (*v*)

*The Côte de Beaune*

The Côte de Beaune is white wine country. Densely planted in Chardonnay, the *Grand Cru* vineyards are responsible for some of the world's richest dry whites, rivaling in fame (and price) the greatest of the red Burgundies.

Although some are quite well-known, the red wine communes rarely approach the superlative qualities of their counterparts in the Côte de Nuits—with the obvious exception of Aloxe-Corton and the vineyard of Le Corton itself, which is capable of producing wines that are unequivocally first rate. The relative softness and earlier maturation of the reds of the Côte de Beaune has earned them an undeniable popularity. Those of the tiny village of Pommard, for example, are so much sought after that their production limits seem stretched almost beyond the limits of credibility.

Central to the Côte de Beaune is the town of Beaune itself, whose existence is largely justified by the presence of numerous Burgundy shippers. These are the companies that buy the production of those many small growers whose fragmented parcels of land have come to blanket the Burgundy landscape. The mainstay of local commerce, reliable Burgundy houses are listed, together with some of the better growers, at the end of this section.

(Exceptional, *e*; very good, *v*; good, *g*.)

**BURGUNDY: The Côte de Beaune**

**TOWN: Aloxe-Corton** (includes **Ladoix-Serrigny**)

Basses Mourettes LS (v)
les Bressandes (e)
les Chaillots (v)
le Charlemagne (e)
les Chaumes (e)
les Chaumes de la Voirosse (e)
le Clos du Roi (e)
les Combes (v)
le Corton (e)
la Coutière LS (v)
les Fournières (v)
les Grandes Lolières LS (v)
les Grèves (e)
les Guérets (v)
les Languettes (e)
les Maréchaudes (v)
les Meix (e)
les Meix Lallemand (e)
en Pauland (e)
les Perrières (e)
Petites Lolières LS (v)
les Piètres (e)
les Pougets (e)
les Renardes (e)
le Rognet et Corton LS (e)
la Toppe-au-Vert LS (v)
les Valozières (v)
les Vercots (v)
les Vergennes LS (e)
Vigne au Saint-Meix (e)

**TOWN: Pernand-Vergelesses**

les Basses Vergelesses (v)
en Caradeux (v)
en Charlemagne (e)
Creux de la Net (v)
les Fichots (v)
Îles des Hauts Vergelesses (v)

**TOWN: Savigny-Les-Beaune**

les Charmières (v)
aux Clous (v)
la Dominode (v)
aux Fourneaux (v)
aux Grands Liards (v)
aux Gravains (v)
aux Guettes (v)
aux Jarrons (v)
les Lavières (v)
aux Marconnets (v)
les Narbantons (v)
Petits Godeaux (v)
aux Petits Liards (v)
les Peuillets (v)
en Redrescul (v)
Ruichottes (v)
aux Serpentières (v)
les Talmettes (v)
aux Vergelesses (v)

**TOWN: Beaune**

les Aigrots (v)
lex Avaux (v)
les Bas des Saucilles (v)
aux Couchéries (v)
aux Crax (v)
Dessus des Marconnets (v)
Pertruisots (v)
les Reversées (v)
les Saucilles (v)

(Exceptional, *e*; very good, *v*; good, *g*.)

BURGUNDY: The Côte de Beaune

TOWN: **Beaune** (cont.)

les Bas des Teurons (*v*)
Belissand (*v*)
les Boucharottes (*v*)
les Boucherottes (*v*)
les Bressandes (*v*)
les Cent Vignes (*v*)
Champs Pimont (*v*)
le Clos de la Mousse (*v*)
Clos du Roi (*v*)

à l'Écu (*v*)
les Epenottes (*v*)
les Fèves (*v*)
en Genet (*v*)
les Grèves (*v*)
sur les Grèves (*v*)
les Marconnets (*v*)
la Mignotte (*v*)
les Montrevenots (*v*)
en Orme (*v*)
les Perrières (*v*)

les Seurey (*v*)
Siserpe (*v*)
les Sizies (*v*)
les Teurons (*v*)
les Theurons (*v*)
Tiélandry (*v*)
les Toussaints (*v*)
les Tuvillains (*v*)
les Vignes Franches (*v*)

TOWN: **Pommard**

les Argillières (*v*)
les Arvelets (*v*)
les Bertins (*v*)
les Boucherottes (*v*)
la Chanière (*v*)
les Chanlins Hauts (*v*)
les Chaponnières (*v*)
les Charmots (*v*)
Clos Blanc (*v*)

Clos de la Commaraine (*v*)
Clos Micot (*v*)
Clos de Verger (*v*)
les Combes Dessus (*v*)
les Croix Noires (*v*)
Derrière Saint Jean (*v*)
les Fremiers (*v*)
les Grands Epenots (*v*)
les Jarollières (*v*)

les Petits Épenots (*v*)
les Pézerolles (*v*)
la Platière (*v*)
les Poutures (*v*)
la Refène (*v*)
les Rugiens (*v*)
les Saucilles (*v*)

TOWN: **Volnay**

les Angles (*v*)
les Aussys (*v*)
la Barre (*v*)

Chantin (*v*)
Clos des Chênes (*v*)
le Clos des Ducs (*v*)

Pointe d'Angles (*v*)
Pousse d'Or (*v*)
Robardelle (*v*)

(Exceptional, *e;* very good, *v;* good, *g.*)

BURGUNDY: The Côte de Beaune

TOWN: **Volnay** (cont.)

Brouillards (*v*)
en Caillerets (*v*)
Caillerets Dessus (*v*)
Carelle Dessous (*v*)
Carelle sous la Chapelle (*v*)
en Champans (*v*)
Frémiots (*v*)
les Lurets (*v*)
les Mitans (*v*)
en l'Ormeau (*v*)
les Pétures (*v*)
Pierres Dessus (*v*)
en Ronceret (*v*)
Santenots (*v*)
Taille Pieds (*v*)
en Verseuil (*v*)
Village de Volnay (*v*)

TOWN: **Monthélie**

les Cas-Rougeot (*v*)
les Champs Fulliot (*v*)
Château Gaillard (*v*)
le Clos Gauthey (*v*)
les Duresses (*v*)
le Meix Bataille (*v*)
les Riottes (*v*)
la Taupine (*v*)
sur Lavelle (*v*)
les Vignes Rondes (*v*)

TOWN: **Auxey-Duresses**

Bas des Duresses (*v*)
les Bretterins (*v*)
la Chapelle (*v*)
les Duresses (*v*)
les Grands Champs (*v*)

TOWN: **Meursault**

sous Blagny (*v*)
les Bouchères (*v*)
les Caillerets (*v*)
les Charmes Dessus (*v*)
les Charmes Dessous (*v*)
les Cras (*v*)
le Dos d'Âne (*v*)
sous le Dos d'Âne (*v*)
les Genevrières Dessus (*v*)
les Genevrières Dessous (*v*)
les Gouttes d'Or (*v*)
la Jennelotte (*v*)
les Perrières Dessous (*v*)
la Pièce sous la Bois (*v*)
les Pétures (*v*)
le Poruzot (*v*)
le Poruzot Dessus (*v*)
le Poruzot Dessous (*v*)
les Santenots Blancs (*v*)
les Santenots du Milieu (*v*)

TOWN: **Puligny-Montrachet**

Bâtard-Montrachet (*v*)
Champ Canet (*v*)
Hameau de Blagny (*v*)

(Exceptional, *e*; very good, *v*; good, *g*.)

BURGUNDY: The Côte de Beaune

**TOWN: Puligny-Montrachet** (cont.)

| | | |
|---|---|---|
| les Bienvenues-Bâtard-Montrachet (*e*) | Chevalier Montrachet (*e*) | les Montrachet (*e*) |
| le Cailleret (*v*) | Clavoillons (*v*) | les Pucelles (*v*) |
| les Chalumeaux (*v*) | les Combettes (*v*) | sous le Puits (*v*) |
| | les Folatières (*v*) | les Referts (*v*) |

**TOWN: Chassagne-Montrachet**

| | | |
|---|---|---|
| Abbaye de Morgeot (*v*) | les Chévenottes (*v*) | la Maltroie (*v*) |
| Bâtard Montrachet (*e*) | Clos Saint Jean (*v*) | les Montrachet (*e*) |
| la Boudriotte (*v*) | les Criots-Bâtard-Montrachet (*e*) | |
| les Brussonnes (*v*) | Grandes Ruchottes en Caillerets (*v*) | Morgeot (*v*) |
| les Champs-Gains (*v*) | les Macherelles (*v*) | la Romanée (*v*) |
| Chassagne (*v*) | | les Vergers (*v*) |

**TOWN: Saint-Aubin**

| | | |
|---|---|---|
| Champlot (*v*) | les Frionnes (*v*) | en Remilly (*v*) |
| la Chatenière (*v*) | sur Gamay (*v*) | sur le Sentier du Clou (*v*) |
| les Combes (*v*) | les Murgers des Dents de Chien (*v*) | |

**TOWN: Santenay**

| | | |
|---|---|---|
| Beauregard (*v*) | la Comme (*v*) | Passe Temps (*v*) |
| Beaurepaire (*v*) | les Gravières (*v*) | |
| Clos des Tavannes (*v*) | la Maladière (*v*) | |

*Chalonnais*

Here is an excellent opportunity for the consumer to enjoy the red and white Burgundy styles, without the Burgundy price. While it could never be claimed that these are great wines, it is difficult to deny them a pleasant and respectable status. Since they have somehow remained quite unknown abroad, their prices have held both appealing and steady.

Pinot Noir and Chardonnay are the legally permissible grapes, best represented in the wines of four towns: Mercurey and Givry for reds; and Rully and Montagny for whites.

*Mâconnais*

With the exception of the odd red (made from Gamay and bottled as Beaujolais), the Mâconnais is almost exclusively a white wine area. The Chardonnay has become popularized here through the remarkable success of Pouilly-Fuissé, a less acidic wine than the whites of the Côte d'Or and notably soft in its youth. Although a little age is still preferable for better bottles, the pressures of the current market have forced Pouilly-Fuissé into regrettably early retirement. Almost every vintage, irrespective of quality, is sold by the following spring or early summer, then shipped across the world for rapid consumption. Excellent values are often to be found in some of the lesser wines of the area, particularly the frequently reliable Mâcon Blanc.

*Beaujolais*

Beaujolais provides the consumer with the wine drinking experience at its simple best. The ideal is not to search for complexities and refinements, but rather to capture the young Gamay aroma in a brilliantly purple, inexpensive wine. For this style of drinking come the *Appellations* of Beaujolais, Beaujolais-Villages and Beaujolais Supérieur.

Within the *Appellation* of Beaujolais, there are nine communes producing wines from the Gamay that cannot be taken as light-heartedly as the rest. Known as the *Crus* (growths) of Beaujolais, they are labeled by commune name and range in character from a slight refinement of the Beaujolais-Villages to a grand Burgundy style that may age for several years in the bottle. In recent years, these wines have not been associated so much with the traditional simplicity of Beaujolais and have risen considerably in price. In fact, a good wine from Fleurie or Moulin-à-Vent may now cost nearly as much as a red Burgundy from the Côte d'Or.

To fully enjoy the lesser wines of Beaujolais, a slight chill is suggested. The *Crus* should be essentially regarded as big red wines: a breathing period of thirty minutes opens them considerably, and they should be served at near room temperature.

BEAUJOLAIS
**Beaujolais Nouveau:** a fresh, grapey wine, made to be consumed immediately after vintage, from the end of November until the following spring. Hurried vinification rapidly renders them unstable. **Beaujolais:** simple, direct country wine, more stable than Nouveau, but its low 9% alcohol will not keep the wine much beyond a year.
**Beaujolais Supérieur:** an additional degree of alcohol raises the *Appellation* to Supérieur.
**Beaujolais-Villages:** second in quality only to the growths. Limited to the finer Beaujolais areas and usually a good value.

*CRUS* (Growths of Beaujolais):
**Brouilly:** its charm lies in its simple, uncomplicated fruitiness.
**Côte de Brouilly:** a Brouilly of particular depth and higher alcohol.
**Morgon:** more body still and requiring several years of bottle age.
**Chiroubles:** although a little heavier than Morgon, nonetheless shorter-lived.
**Fleurie:** the most refined of the Beaujolais, benefiting from a good 2 or 3 years in the bottle.
**Moulin-à-Vent:** gaining from longer on-skin fermentation, and decidedly big.
**Chénas:** similar to Moulin-à-Vent, but not quite as powerful.
**Juliénas:** lush, forward wines, higher than Chénas in the obvious qualities of fruit.
**St.-Amour:** adds body to the Beaujolais concept of simple, light drinking.

## BURGUNDY
### RELIABLE PRODUCERS:

P.A. André
Bouchard Père & Fils
André Brunet
Caves de la Busserolle

Chanson Père & Fils
Clair Dâu
Félix Clerget
Joseph Drouhin
Drouhin-Laroze
Duc de Magenta
J. Faiveley
Domaine Fleurot-Larose
Hospices de Beaune

Louis Jadot
Hubert Lamy
Jean Lamy & ses Fils
Louis Latour

Domaine Leflaive
Leroy S.A.
de Lupé-Cholet
Domaine Marey-Monge
Marquis de Laguiche
Pierre Matrot
Moillard
Patriarche Père & Fils
Pierre Ponnelle

Poulet Père & Fils
Ramonet-Prudhon
Rapet Père & Fils
Domaine de la Romanée-
    Conti
Ropiteau Frères
Étienne Sauzet
Baron Thenard
Roland Thévenin
Charles Vienot
Léon Violland
Comte Georges de Vogüé

## BURGUNDY VINTAGES
*(as of 1977)*

1976 A good year throughout, especially in the Côte d'Or. Sales slowed by particularly high opening prices.

1975 A near disaster. A late-harvest hail drastically reduced the size of vintage. The whites have seemingly fared best.

1974 Not a big year.

1973 A large crop of relatively light wines made for good prices.

1972 While the wines are still hard, a good deal of fruit is showing through. If their acidity is shed gracefully, this could be a good year.

1971 A great year, but very few are now available. This is the sort of Burgundy that is genuinely worth laying down for several years yet.

1970 Early maturing and rich. They are still good, but to find them might be difficult.

1969 A low yield of very good wines. The big ones are just beginning to come around.

The current style of Burgundy assumes optimum aging periods of five to seven years for excellent vintages and three to four for lesser ones. Old Burgundies are difficult to come by: when they do show up, their state of maturity may well prove disappointing.

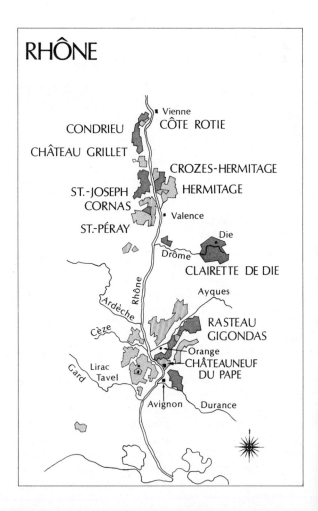

RHÔNE

CONDRIEU

CHÂTEAU GRILLET

Vienne
CÔTE ROTIE

CROZES-HERMITAGE

ST.-JOSEPH
CORNAS

HERMITAGE

ST.-PÉRAY

Valence

Die

Drôme

CLAIRETTE DE DIE

Ayques

Ardèche

Rhône

RASTEAU
GIGONDAS

Cèze

Orange

Lirac
Tavel

CHÂTEAUNEUF
DU PAPE

Gard

Avignon    Durance

## THE RHÔNE

Wine making in the Rhône is the activity of two distinct districts, which can be referred to quite simply as the North and the South. Although many of the same grapes are grown in both areas, the North exhibits a strong tendency toward the production of long-lived wines that deserve the careful attention of the consumer, while the South is known more for its soft, easy-to-drink dinner wines. All are high in alcohol and usually dependent on more than one grape, the blends often becoming outrageously complex.

Throughout the Rhône, there are vineyards of sufficient importance to justify estate bottling and to warrant the interest of shippers. In fact many a shipper as far away as Beaune will round off his price list with the famous Châteauneuf-du-Pape, Tavel, Hermitage, and an inexpensive Côtes du Rhône. Those houses that are based in the Rhône itself often tend to be especially sensitive to the treatment of local wines. It remains true, however, that the product of a single known estate is universally preferable and, until they become more widely-known, there is little difference in cost.

The Côtes du Rhône is the only *Appellation* that embraces the production of the entire area, its reds, whites, and rosés made on both sides of the river, from just south of Lyon to below Avignon. Their principal interest for the export market lies in the reds, which are the frequent offerings of a broad range of shippers. The *Appellation* is a simple one and rarely conducive to estate bottling: what few estates there are tend to be both good and reliable. It is not easy to make any sensible generalizations about the grapes of the area, except to state that there are at least fifteen varieties in common use. We can assume the better reds to be reasonably strong in Grenache or Syrah.

*The North*

Côte Rotie is the first *Appellation* encountered on the road south from Lyon. Here, a particularly delicate red wine is produced from the vines of two separate slopes, the Syrah from the Côte Brune (a dark-skinned grape, used in the production of red wine) and the Viognier from the Côte Blonde (used normally for whites). It is a common practice of Rhône vintners to mellow their powerful reds with a small amount of white wine, a principle that is largely responsible for the attractive balance of the Côtes Roties. These are wines that improve significantly with age but, in most export situations, are seldom allowed to reach their peak.

In Condrieu, it is the Viognier that is responsible for an interesting, flowery style of white with an exciting, dry finish. Unfortunately, its production is both small and expensive, and its distribution severely limited. Château Grillet, the best of the Condrieux, is sufficiently distinctive to justify its own *Appellation*.

Further to the south, we come to Cornas and St.-Joseph, known mostly for their good, sound red wines. Of greater importance, however, is their neighbor, Hermitage, on the opposite side of the river.

Hermitage is alone in rivaling Côte Rotie as the finest of the Rhône reds, but the two are distinguished by such radically different styles that the challenge is hardly fair. Hermitage starts out as a big, almost coarse wine but, with a little age, it begins to take on a complexity that is entirely its own.

As so often happens in the wine regions of France, a nearby commune has made use of the hyphen to increase the popularity of its wines. While its price is not too far from that of an Hermitage, a wine from Crozes-Hermitage is seldom more impressive than a big red from the Côtes du Rhône.

St.-Péray is the least important of the northern Rhône *Appellations*. Its whites are big, but usually too high in alcohol and too sweet to emerge with any real measure of subtlety. They are occasionally made *mousseux* (sparkling).

*The South*

The wines of the southern Rhône are clustered around the town of Orange, in the *départements* of Vaucluse, Gard, and Drôme. The Côtes du Rhône-Villages, whose status is slightly higher than that of the Côtes du Rhône, are all located in the South. Here, the appropriate town name will appear on the label in addition to an *Appellation* statement for the Côtes du Rhône. Gigondas, one of the original towns, has recently been awarded its own *Appellation*, and it seems likely that the privilege will be extended to include the others.

There is little doubt that the best red wines of the South originate in Châteauneuf-du-Pape. In this one *Appellation,* no less than thirteen grape varieties are legally permitted, the individual *domaines* (estates) informally indentified by their respective blends. A combination of several of the following is possible: Syrah, Grenache, Cinsault, Mourvèdre, Muscardin, Vaccarèse, Counoïse, Picpoule, Clairette, Bourboulenc, Terret Noir, Picardin, and Rousanne.

Much shipper wine is produced in the area, although the best remains in the hands of the *domaines* (those that are recommended are tabulated at the end of this section). With the exception of the wealthiest estates, the wines undergo very little barrel age and can be enjoyed in the early stages of their development. But even these, with all their alcohol and ruggedness, can still age respectably in the bottle and may survive a good ten, or even fifteen years. With time in the wood, they may last even longer.

Although the home of some rather heavy, sweetish reds, Tavel and Lirac are known mostly for their good Grenache rosés. Tavel is by far the sturdier of the two and may age impressively for five to seven years, a longevity that is entirely exceptional in the world of rosé. The softer Liracs are better confined to local consumption.

*Recommended vintages (as of 1977):* 1976, 1974, 1973, and 1972.

(Exceptional, *e*; very good, *v*; good, *g*.)

## RHÔNE
### RED

| | | |
|---|---|---|
| Cornas (*v*) | St. Joseph (*v*) | Gigondas (*v*) |
| Côte Rôtie (*e*) | Lirac (*g*) | |
| Hermitage (*e*) | Crozes-Hermitage (*g*) | |

### WHITE

| | | |
|---|---|---|
| Condrieu (*e*) | Châteauneuf-du-Pape (*v*) | Côtes du Rhône (*g*) |
| Château Grillet (*e*) | St. Péray (*g*) | |
| Hermitage (*e*) | St. Péray Mousseux (*g*) | |

### ROSÉ

| | |
|---|---|
| Tavel (*v*) | Lirac (*g*) |

## CÔTES DU RHÔNE-VILLAGES
### RED

| | | |
|---|---|---|
| Beaumes-de-Venise (*v*) | Roaix (*v*) | Vacqueras |
| Cairanne (*v*) | Rochegude (*v*) | Valréas |
| Chusclan (*v*) | St.-Maurice-sur-Eygues | Vinsobres |
| Laudun (*v*) | St. Pantaleon-les-Vignes | Visan |
| Rasteau (*v*) | Séguret | |

## CHÂTEAUNEUF-DU-PAPE

| | | |
|---|---|---|
| Domaine de Beaurenard (*e*) | Château Fortia (*e*) | Clos des Papes (*e*) |
| Les Brusquières (*e*) | Château de la Gardine (*e*) | Clos Saint-Jean (*e*) |
| Château des Fines Roches (*e*) | Château Maucoil (*e*) | Domaine de la Solitude (*e*) |
| La Font du Loup (*e*) | Domaine de Mont-Redon (*e*) | |
| | Domaine de la Nerte (*e*) | |

# BORDEAUX

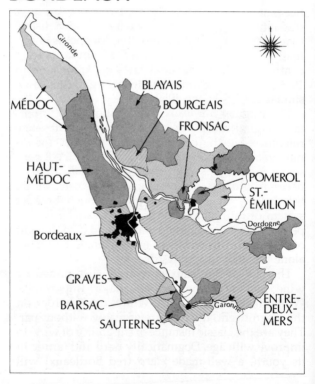

## BORDEAUX

The merchants of Bordeaux are an evolved professional community ordered by categories of their
own invention. As early as the thirteenth century,
wines were being "shipped" in quantity from local
English holdings to the ports of Bristol and
Southampton, thus establishing a commercial practice that is the genesis of the modern trade. By 1855,
the status of each vineyard was so well-established
that a large area of Bordeaux (the Médoc) was for-
mally classified by quality. Internal standards were
confirmed by the national laws of *Appellation* in
1936, and areas beyond the Médoc began their own
similar ratings in the 1950s.

The original Bordeaux classifications are important, both historically and in terms of absolute
reference, but the passing of time has brought in-
numerable changes to the vineyard scene. As a consumer reference guide, the 1855 classification is
necessarily dated and occasionally obsolete. In the
lists below, we have attempted a much broader
system of rating based on market availability and
personal experience. In no way should it be thought
of as an effort to reclassify even a single estate, let
alone the enormity of Bordeaux.

The city of Bordeaux is entirely surrounded by
wine making communes of major importance.
While their sweet and dry whites often border on
the magnificent, the reds are arguably without par.
They are the classic instance of the ability of wine to
improve with age. Dogmatically hard and tannic in
its youth, a well-made *claret* (red Bordeaux) will

gracefully mature to a level of almost indescribable complexity. Prices are compounded steeply with time, and there is every reason to recommend the early purchase of reliable bottlings from good vintages for consumption at a (considerably) later date.

Almost all Bordeaux worthy of consideration is château-bottled. While the established estates are justifiably never cheap, some excellent châteaux are frequently available for little more than we might expect to pay for one of the better California varietals. A considered experiment is rarely disappointing.

In the pages that follow, we have attempted a comprehensive description of the major communes of Bordeaux. We should bear in mind, however, that this group occupies only a limited part of the enormous total production of regional Bordeaux. Although less well-known on the American market, several other *Appellations* are consistently responsible for a number of good table wines. In the Haut-Médoc, Moulis is perhaps best represented by Château Chasse-Spleen, Ludon by Château La Lagune, and Macau by Château Cantemerle. Elsewhere, decent red wines are produced in Bergerac, Bourg, and Blaye, while Entre-Deux-Mers and Monbazillac have become known for a broad range of enjoyable whites.

*St.-Estèphe (Haut-Médoc)*

The northernmost commune of the Haut-Médoc (a major strip of land, north of Bordeaux) is St.-Estèphe. It is also one of the four most famous, having within its *Appellation* many of the original classified growths of 1855. As we travel up-river on the Gironde from the Atlantic coast, St.-Estèphe is the first commune we encounter that offers the appropriate combination of gravelly soil and well-drained slopes to allow for the production of quality wine.

Along with the archetypal Médoc tendency toward a high concentration of tannins, the wines of St.-Estèphe verge on an almost uncompromising dryness. In better vintages, they require a good five to eight years of bottle age before any real signs of maturity become apparent. Styles range from the relatively light, but hard Château Calon-Ségur to the much fruitier and heavier Montrose.

While Cabernet Sauvignon is the principal grape of the area, the other Médoc varieties (Merlot, Petit Verdot, and Cabernet Franc) are used almost everywhere in minor proportions.

(Exceptional, e; very good, v; good, g.)

**BORDEAUX: St.-Estèphe**
Ch. Andron-Blanquet, St. Roch (g)
Ch. Beauséjour, Picard (g)
Ch. Beau-Site (g)
Ch. Bel-Air (g)
Cru Bontemps (g)
Ch. Bournac (g)
Cru des Cachères (g)
Ch. Calon-Ségur (v)
Ch. Canteloup (g)
Ch. Capbern (g)
Ch. Capbern-Gasqueton (g)
Ch. La Rose Capbern (g)
Ch. Grand-Village Capbern (g)
Ch. Chambert (Marbuzet) (g)
Clos Castets, Ch. St. Seurin
Ch. Clauzet (g)
Ch. de Côme (g)
Ch. Cos d'Estournel (v)
Ch. Cos Labory (v)
Ch. Coutelin Merville (g)
Ch. Domeyne (g)
Ch. Eyquem (g)
Ch. Fatin (g)

Clos de Ferrand (g)
Cru des Fines Graves (g)
Cru du Grand Rullong (g)
Ch. Hanteillan (g)
Ch. Haut Coutelin (g)
Ch. Haut Hagna (g)
Ch. Haut La Tour de Coutelin (g)
Ch. Haut Marbuzet (g)
Ch. Haut Verdon (g)
Ch. Hostein (g)
Ch. Houissant (g)
Cru La Chapelle (g)
Ch. Ladouys (g)
Ch. Laffitte-Carcasset (g)
Ch. Lafon-Rochet (v)
Ch. Lartigue (g)
Ch. La Tour Brana (g)
Ch. La Tour Coutelin (g)
Ch. la Tour du Haut Vignoble (g)
Ch. La Tour de Leyssac (g)
Ch. La Tour Lichine (g)
Ch. La Tour de Marbuzet (g)
Ch. La Tour des Ternes (g)
Ch. Le Boscq (g)

Ch. Le Crock (g)
Ch. Le Roc (g)
Ch. Les Ormes-de-Pez (g)
Ch. l'Hôpital (g)
Ch. Marbuzet (g)
Ch. Meyney (g)
Ch. Montrose (v)
Ch. Morin (g)
Ch. Moulin-de-Calon (g)
Clos du Moulin (g)
Cru Muscadet (g)
Ch. Palmer (g)
Ch. de Pez (g)
Ch. Phélan-Ségur (g)
Ch. Plantier-Rose (g)
Cru Poumarin (g)
Cru des Pradines (g)
Domaine des Pradines (g)
Cru Ribeau (g)
Ch. St-Estèphe (g)
Ch. St.-Estèphe 'la Croix' (g)
Cru Taste (g)
Ch. Tronquoy-Lalande (g)
Cru du Troupian (g)

*Pauillac (Haut-Médoc)*

The wines of Pauillac (immediately to the south of
St.-Estèphe, likewise bordering on the western bank
of the Gironde) are something of a delight to the
professional taster. The complex blends of Cabernet
Sauvignon, Petit Verdot, Merlot, and Cabernet
Franc would seem to offer almost limitless possibili-
ties within a single commune. Pauillac is also home
to three *Premier Grand Cru* vineyards, the very
highest of the Bordeaux ratings. Château Lafite-
Rothschild, followed closely by Mouton-Rothschild
and Latour, is annually responsible for establishing
standards of market value for every wine in Bordeaux. Not only are these the greatest of the
Pauillacs, they also rank as some of the finest red
wines in the world.

The geographically superior vineyards occur at
the highest altitudes to optimize critical drainage.
The soil, which is deep gravel, is of little use for
crops other than the vine, although it is not easy to
think of a more financially rewarding endeavour.

**BORDEAUX: Pauillac**
Ch. Balogues-Haut-Bages (g)
Ch. Batailley (v)
Ch. Clerc-Milon-Mondon (v)
Ch. Croizet-Bages (v)
Ch. Duhart-Milon-
Rothschild (v)
Ch. Fonbadet (g)
Ch. Grand-Puy-Ducasse (v)
Ch. Grand-Puy-Lacoste (v)
Ch. Haut Bages Libéral (v)
Ch. Haut-Bages-Monpelou (g)
Ch. Haut-Batailley (v)
Ch. Haut Daubos (g)
Ch. La Couronne (g)
Ch. Lafite-Rothschild (e)

Ch. Lafleur Milon (g)
Ch. La Gravière-Haut-
Bages (g)
Ch. Latour (e)
Ch. La Tour d'Anseillan (g)
Ch. La Tour d'Aspic (g)
Ch. La Tour Duroch
Milon (g)
Ch. La Tour Pibran (g)
Ch. Lynch-Bages (v)
Ch. Lynch-Moussas (v)
Ch. Malécot (g)
Ch. Milon-Mousset (g)
Ch. Mongrand-Milon (g)
Ch. Monpelou (g)

(Exceptional, *e;* very good, *v;* good, *g.)*
Ch. Moulin de la
Bridane (g)
Ch. Mouton-Rothschild (e)
Ch. Mouton-Baron
Philippe (v)
Ch. Pédesclaux (v)
Ch. Pibran (g)
Ch. Pichon-Lalande (v)
Ch. Pichon-Longue-
ville (v)
Ch. Plaisance (g)
Ch. Pontet-Canet (v)
Ch. Roland (g)
Clos St. Martin (g)

*St.-Julien (Haut-Médoc)*

South of Pauillac is the commune of St.-Julien, possessing no *Premiers Crus* from the 1855 classification but no less than a third of the fifteen Second Growths. While it is a small *Appellation,* the concentration of important châteaux is remarkably high, and its wines are no less attractive than those from competing areas within Bordeaux.

Two châteaux in particular have shown tremendous improvement since the original classification, namely, Gloria and Beychevelle. To a slightly lesser extent, the same is also true of Talbot, which would certainly rank higher than its present Fourth Growth status in any modern assessment.

In character, the wines of St.-Julien fall midway between the hardness of the Pauillacs and the almost universal softness of the Margaux. With the exception of the very best, they are perceptibly lighter than most other Médocs, and they mature rather more rapidly.

BORDEAUX: **St.-Julien**
Cru Arnaud (g)
Ch. Beauregard (g)
Cru le Bécasse du
    Ferrey (g)
Ch. Beychevelle (v)
Ch. Bontemps-DuBarry (g)
Ch. Branaire-Ducru (v)
Ch. du Brassat (g)
Ch. Ducru-Beaucaillou (v)
Ch. Ferrey Gros Caillou (g)

Ch. du Glana (g)
Ch. Gloria (v)
Ch. Grand St.-Julien (g)
Ch. Gruaud-Larose (v)
Ch. Laconfourgue (g)
Ch. Lagrange (v)
Ch. Langoa (v)
Ch. La Rose de France (g)
Ch. Léoville-Barton (v)
Ch. Léoville-Las-Cases (v)

(Exceptional, e; very good, v; good, g.)
Ch. Léoville-Poyferré (v)
Clos du Marquis (g)
Ch. Moulin de la Rose (g)
Ch. Moulin-Riche (g)
Clos St.-Julien (g)
Ch. St.-Louis-Dubosq (g)
Ch. Saint-Pierre (v)
Ch. Talbot (v)
Ch. Terrey Gros Caillou (g)
Ch. Teynac (g)

*Margaux (Haut-Médoc)*
Margaux is separated from St.-Julien by a distance
of more than five miles and a grouping of minor
Central Médoc areas. The *Appellation* of Margaux
actually extends to four communes beyond
Margaux itself: Cantenac, Soussans, Arsac, and
Labarde are all entitled to that one *Appellation*,
which represents the most southerly of the major
regions embraced by the limits of the Haut-Médoc.

The most famous estate is that of Château
Margaux, which joins Lafite et al. as a First Growth.
We feel Château Palmer to be its closest current
rival, deserving far greater recognition than might
be expected from what is only a Third Growth.

There is a special softness, even fragility about
Margaux wines, which sets them distinctly apart
from almost every other wine in Bordeaux. This is
something of a detriment in poor years, when
unripe fruit might have a little difficulty in surviv-
ing the complex process of aging.

There remains, however, a generous share of
above-average wines, and good values are apparent
in every commune. Interestingly enough, Margaux
would seem to produce the best of the regionally-
bottled Bordeaux.

**BORDEAUX: Margaux**

(Exceptional, *e;* very good, *v;* good, *g.*)

Ch. l'Abbégorsse-de-
  Gorsse (*g*)
Ch. Angludet (*g*)
Ch. Baraillot (*g*)
Ch. Bel-Air-Marquis
  d'Aligre (*g*)
Ch. Bellevue-les-Haut-
  Graves (*g*)
Ch. Boyd-Cantenac (*v*)
Ch. Brane-Cantenac (*e*)
Domaine de Campion (*g*)
Ch. Cantenac-Brown (*v*)
Cru Cougot (*g*)
Ch. Curé-Bourse (*g*)
Ch. Dauzac (*v*)
Ch. Desmirail (*v*)
Ch. Deyrim-Valentin (*g*)
Ch. Durfort-Vivens (*v*)
Ch. Ferrière (*v*)
Ch. Giscours (*v*)
Ch. Grand-Jaugeyron (*g*)
Ch. Grand-Soussans (*g*)
Ch. Cru du Gravier (*g*)
Ch. d'Issan (*v*)
Ch. Kirwan (*v*)
Ch. Labégorce (*g*)
Ch. Labégorce-Zédé (*g*)
Ch. La Colomilla (*g*)
Ch. La Galiane (*g*)
Ch. La Gombaude (*g*)
Ch. La Gurgue (*g*)
Ch. Lamouroux (*g*)
Ch. de Laroze (*g*)
Ch. Lascombes (*v*)
Ch. La Tour-de-Bessan (*g*)
Ch. La Tour de Mons (*g*)
Ch. Malescot-Saint-
  Exupéry (*v*)
Ch. Margaux (*e*)
Ch. Marquis d'Alesme-
  Becker (*v*)
Ch. Marquis de Terme (*v*)
Ch. Marsac-Sequineau (*g*)
Ch. Martinens (*g*)
Ch. Montbrun (*g*)
Ch. Palmer (*e*)
Ch. Pauzac (*g*)
Ch. Paveil (*g*)
Ch. Pontet Chappez (*g*)
Ch. Pouget (*v*)
Ch. Prieuré-Lichine (*v*)
Ch. Rauzan-Gassies (*v*)
Ch. Rausan-Ségla (*v*)
Ch. Richeterre (*g*)
Cru Richet-Marian (*g*)
Cru St. Pierre (*g*)
Ch. Siran (*g*)
Ch. Tayac-Plaisance (*g*)
Ch. du Tertre (*v*)
Ch. Vallière (*g*)
Ch. Vincent (*g*)

*Graves*

The greatest of the Graves estates, Châteaux Haut-Brion and La Mission Haut-Brion, are actually located within the suburbs of the city of Bordeaux, while the remaining *Appellation* stretches immediately to the south to include the smaller communes of Pessac, Martillac, and Léognan. Although not a part of the Médoc, it is interesting to note that the standing of Haut-Brion in 1855 was sufficiently impressive to warrant its classification as a *Premier Grand Cru.*

Much Graves, especially the white wines, goes directly to Bordeaux under a simple regional label for café and restaurant consumption. The château-bottled whites, made mostly from Sémillion and Sauvignon Blanc, are often particularly enjoyable, with a powerful fruitiness in a good year that imparts an almost flowery first impression, followed by an aftertaste that is long and dry. If we were to compare them with a white Burgundy, we might find the Graves somewhat lighter in body, but in a pleasant, subdued fashion.

The reds, on the other hand, are enormous and long-lived, with a certain underlying earthiness that is attractive even in their youth, and a source of power and complexity in their maturity.

(Exceptional, *e*; very good, *v*; good *g*.)

## BORDEAUX: Graves

### RED

Ch. Baret (*v*)
Ch. Bahans (*v*)
Ch. Bouscaut (*v*)
Ch. Carbonnieux (*v*)
Domaine de Chevalier (*v*)
Ch. Fieuzal (*v*)

Ch. Haut-Bailly (*v*)
Ch. Haut-Brion (*e*)
Ch. La Mission-Haut-Brion (*e*)
Ch. La Tour Haut-Brion (*v*)
La Tour Martillac (*v*)

Ch. Malartic-Lagravière (*v*)
Ch. Olivier (*v*)
Ch. Pape-Clément (*e*)
Ch. Smith-Haut-Lafitte (*v*)

### WHITE

Ch. Baret (*v*)
Ch. Bouscaut (*v*)
Ch. Carbonnieux (*v*)
Domaine de Chevalier (*e*)

Ch. Couhins (*e*)
Ch. Latour Martillac (*v*)
Ch. Laville-Haut-Brion (*e*)
Ch. Malartic-Lagravière (*e*)

Ch. Olivier (*e*)
Ch. Haut-Brion Blanc (*e*)

*Sauternes and Barsac*

The wines of Sauternes and Barsac (Barsac is a commune within the general area of Sauternes, some thirty miles south-east of Bordeaux) owe many of their very special qualities to the action of a mold, known locally as *pourriture noble,* or Noble Rot *(Botrytis Cinerea).* Formed late in the growing season on the skins of ripe grapes, *Botrytis* causes a rapid shriveling of the fruit to increase the concentration of sugars and acids. The Mediterranean practice of simply drying the grapes in the sun would have entirely the same effect were it not for the tendency of *Botrytis* to attack and reduce the malic and tartaric acid content of the grape. The result is a remarkable harmony of pure sweetness with a hint of retained citric acid. In a good vintage, the young wines start out with the color of pale gold and the almost overpowering taste of simple sugar. With maturity, their pigment deepens as the tannins oxidize, and their sweetness mellows in favor of the true *Botrytis* complexity.

Since *Botrytis* will only infect a limited number of grapes under certain, special conditions, harvesting becomes a matter of enormous care. The sheer lack of liquid in the fruit further reduces the vine's potential yield to firmly establish Sauternes (along with the late-picked, botrytized Germans) in those spectacular realms of costly luxury.

**BORDEAUX: Sauternes and Barsac**          (Exceptional, *e*; very good, *v*; good, *g*.)

Ch. d'Arche (*v*)
Ch. Broustet (*v*)
Ch. Caillou (*v*)
Ch. Climens (*v*)
Ch. Coutet (*v*)
Ch. Doisy-Daëne (*v*)
Ch. Doisy-Védrines (*v*)
Ch. Filhot (*v*)
Ch. Guiraud (*v*)

Clos Haut-Peyraguey (*v*)
Ch. Lafaurie-Peyraguey (*v*)
Ch. Lafon (*g*)
Ch. Lamothe (*v*)
Ch. La Tour Blanche (*e*)
Ch. de Malle (*v*)
Ch. Myrat (*v*)
Ch. Nairac (*v*)

Ch. Rabaud-Promis (*v*)
Ch. Rabaud-Sigalas (*v*)
Ch. Rayne-Vigneau (*e*)
Ch. Rieussec (*e*)
Ch. Romer (*v*)
Ch. Suau (*v*)
Ch. de Suduiraut (*v*)
Ch. d'Yquem (*e*)

### St.-Émilion

In appearance, the old town of St.-Émilion (located a good twenty miles east of the Bordeaux city limits) satisfies the most romantic images of the visiting devotee. Narrow lanes, bordered by the properties of prestigious estates, wind their way lazily toward the steep hills of yellow stone that are the medieval entity of St.-Émilion. The pre-eminence of Merlot produces an attractive, soft style of wine that is surprisingly long-lived, despite its early maturity. The early-ripening properties of Merlot are further responsible for a relatively high proportion of good vintages.

### Pomerol

Pomerol (adjacent to St.-Émilion, near the town of Libourne) is a very small *Appellation* of early-maturing, high quality wines. Their distinguishing characteristics are mostly tactile: they are heavier and softer in the mouth than the wines of the Médoc but slightly less substantial than those of St.-Émilion. (It is interesting to note that Château Cheval-Blanc is not only the best of the wines of St.-Émilion, but also the closest estate to Pomerol.) Although Pomerol has never been officially classified, Château Pétrus consistently emerges as the best, and prices are universally high.

(Exceptional, *e*; very good, *v*; good, *g*.)

**BORDEAUX: St.-Émilion**

Ch. l'Angélus (*g*)
Ch. l'Arrosée (*g*)
Ch. Ausone (*e*)
Ch. Balestard-La-
  Tonnelle (*g*)
Ch. Beauséjour-Duffau-
  Lagarrosse (*v*)
Ch. Beauséjour Fagouet (*v*)
Ch. Belair (*v*)
Ch. Bellevue (*g*)
Ch. Bergat (*g*)
Ch. Cadet-Bon (*g*)
Ch. Cadet-Piolat (*g*)
Ch. Canon (*v*)
Ch. Canon-La-Gaffelière (*g*)
Ch. Cap de Mourlin (*g*)
Ch. la Carte (*g*)
Ch. Chapelle Madeleine (*g*)
Ch. Chatelet (*g*)
Ch. Chauvin (*g*)
Ch. Cheval-Blanc (*e*)
Ch. la Clotte (*g*)
Ch. la Cluzière (*g*)
Ch. Corbin (*g*)
Ch. Corbin-Michotte (*g*)
Ch. Coutet (*g*)

Ch. Croque-Michotte (*g*)
Ch. Curé-Bon (*g*)
Ch. la Dominique (*g*)
Ch. Figeac (*v*)
Ch. Fonplégade (*g*)
Ch. Fonroque (*g*)
Clos Fourtet (*v*)
Ch. Franc-Mayne (*g*)
Ch. Gaffelière-Naudes (*v*)
Ch. Grand-Barrail-
  Lamarzelle-Figeac (*g*)
Ch. Grand-Corbin (*g*)
Ch. Grand-Corbin-
  Despagne (*g*)
Ch. les Grandes
  Murailles (*g*)
Ch. Grand-Mayne (*g*)
Ch. Grand Pontet (*g*)
Ch. Guadet-St.-Julien (*g*)
Clos des Jacobins (*g*)
Ch. Jean Faure (*g*)
Ch. Larcis-Ducasse (*g*)
Ch. Larmande (*g*)
Ch. Laroze (*g*)
Ch. Lasserre (*g*)
Ch. La Tour-Figeac (*g*)

Ch. Madeleine (*g*)
Ch. Magdelaine (*v*)
Ch. la Marzelle (*g*)
Ch. Mauvezin (*g*)
Ch. Moulin-du-Cadet (*g*)
Ch. Pavie (*v*)
Ch. Pavie-Decesse (*g*)
Ch. Pavie-Macquin (*g*)
Ch. Pavillon-Cadet (*g*)
Ch. Petit-Faurie-de-
  Soutard (*g*)
Ch. Petit-Faurie-de-
  Souchard (*g*)
Ch. Le Prieuré (*g*)
Ch. Ripeau (*g*)
Ch. St.-Georges-Côte-
  Pavie (*g*)
Ch. St.-Martin (*g*)
Ch. Sansonnet (*g*)
Ch. Soutard (*g*)
Ch. Tertre-Daugay (*g*)
Ch. Trimoulet (*g*)
Ch. Trois-Moulins (*g*)
Ch. Troplong-Mondot (*g*)
Ch. Trottevielle (*v*)
Ch. Villemaurine (*v*)

BORDEAUX: **St.-Émilion**

Ch. la Couspaude (*g*)
Ch. Le Couvent (*g*)

Ch. La Tour-du-Pin-
Figeac (*g*)

(Exceptional, *e*; very good, *v*; good, *g*.)
Ch. Yon-Figeac (*g*)

Other communes having the right to bear the St.-Émilion *Appellation*: St.-Georges-St.-Émilion, Montagne-St.-Émilion, Lussac-St.-Émilion, Puisseguin-St.-Émilion, Parsac-St.-Émilion.

BORDEAUX: **Pomerol**

Ch. Beauregard (*v*)
Ch. Certan-de-May (*v*)
Ch. Certan-Giraud (*v*)
Clos de l'Eglise-Clinet (*v*)
Domaine de l'Eglise (*v*)
Ch. l'Evangile (*e*)
Ch. Gazin (*e*)
Ch. La Cabanne (*g*)

Ch. La Conseillante (*e*)
Ch. La Croix (*v*)
Ch. La Fleur (*v*)
Ch. Lafleur-Pétrus (*v*)
Ch. Lagrange (*v*)
Ch. La Pointe (*v*)
Ch. Latour-Pomerol (*v*)
Ch. Nénin (*v*)

Ch. Petit-Village (*e*)
Ch. Pétrus (*e*)
Ch. Rouget (*v*)
Ch. de Sales (*v*)
Ch. Tailhas (*v*)
Ch. Trotanoy (*v*)
Vieux-Château-Certan (*e*)

### BORDEAUX VINTAGES
*(as of 1977)*

1976  The Bordeaux vintners have been comparing these to the 1967s. A fruity, early maturing year is expected.

1975  Along with 1970, this is the best year currently available for laying down. Good fruit and acid balance, but showing no signs of early drinkability.

1974  Decidedly underrated. Of good quality and still very affordable.

1973  A light and fruity year for most areas. Some are currently drinking well, but should be considerably improved by 1980.

1972  Generally disappointing.

1971  Showing much acid at present, but little fruit. Enthusiastic early endorsements may prove rash: the hardness of certain years never seems to mellow.

1970  A fat, fruity year that may come around quicker than expected. Some are already beginning to brick.

1969  Not recommended.

1968  A failure.

1967  Originally hailed as early-maturing, the 1967s were supposed to have been drunk young. After ten years, however, they are still doing splendidly and do not seem at all fragile.

Before purchasing older vintages, we should satisfy ourselves, as far as it is possible, as to the history of the wines' storage. Very old wine is inescapably a risk. The following are recommended: 1966 (still young), 1964 (mostly for St.-Émilions and Pomerols), 1962, and 1961 (great). Still older vintages are even rarer: 1959, 1955, 1953, 1952, 1949, 1947, 1945, 1929, and 1928.

### THE LOIRE VALLEY

Of France's principal table wine districts, the Loire Valley lies closest to Paris. With their simple charm and easy availability, the wines of the Loire have traveled beyond the cafés and restaurants of the French capital to the wine consuming countries of the world.

The River Loire rises some fifty miles west of the Rhône, on a latitude just south of Lyon. From its source it flows northwards until it reaches Pouilly-sur-Loire, the first wine town of major importance. After Pouilly it runs generally to the west, its often exquisite banks populated with vines and country houses all the way to the Atlantic coast.

Beginning with Pouilly-sur-Loire, we come upon wines made from the Chasselas grape, while its neighbor, Sancerre, is planted in Sauvignon Blanc. Both are tart whites and are known by their town names, with the exception of the white Pouilly-Fumé, which is made from Sauvignon Blanc (and is entirely separate from the Pouilly-Fuissé of the Mâconnais). Harder, but otherwise similar wines are made in the areas of Quincy and Reuilly on the River Cher, which at this point runs parallel and to the west of the Loire.

The next *Appellation* is that of Vouvray, near the town of Tours. Here the legal grape is Chenin Blanc, whose style of wine will vary enormously with the decision of the vintner. Vouvray can range from a dry fruitiness to a late-picked, almost dessert delight, with various popular categories of semi-sweetness in between. The sweeter versions age particularly well in the bottle, gaining in complexity as their color deepens to gold and their sweetness mellows. Similar wines are made directly across the river from Vouvray, just south of Montlouis.

Broadly surrounding Vouvray are the Coteaux de Touraine, whose white, red, and rosé wines offer the consumer an easy, soft drinkability. The area contains two villages of major importance, Bourgeuil and Chinon, where the Cabernet Franc is made into those attractive, fresh reds that do so well with light meats and poultry.

Continuing to the west, we come to Saumur, Anjou, and the Coteaux du Layon. With the possible exception of Tavel from the Rhône, this is perhaps the only area in the world capable of producing rosés of distinction—assuming such a phenomenon exists. The slightly crackling rosés of Saumur often provide a little fun, while the familiar Rosé d'Anjou has become the most widely exported wine of the Loire. Deeper hues of pink are often the work of the Cabernet Franc, whose presence is clearly indicated on the label.

Of far greater importance, however, are the white wines of the area, often reserved for the palate and pocketbook of the extravagant connoisseur. Right along the river, close to Savennières, the tiny vineyard of La Coulée de Serrant makes splendid dry whites with the body and flavor of honey, minus the sweetness. Similar in style are the wines of the less romantic La Roche aux Moines. The whites of the Coteaux du Layon are characteristically sweet, and emerge, in the case of the

Quarts de Chaume and Bonnezeaux, as dessert wines of undisputed excellence. Here is Chenin Blanc at its unrivaled best.

Closer now to Nantes and the Loire estuary, we arrive at the extensive vineyards of Muscadet. As less expensive alternatives to the dry whites of Chablis and the Côte d'Or, Muscadets have fared particularly well in the white wine boom of the '70s. Slightly softer and lower in alcohol than the wines of Burgundy, Muscadets remain a distinctly good value.

In general, the wines of the Loire have held steady at attractive prices, offering the consumer a wide spectrum of appealing buys. Increasing popularity, however, and the constant possibility of price increases in low-yield years might suggest that the good old days of a bargain 'round every corner will soon have passed into the realms of fond memories.

(Exceptional, *e*; very good, *v*; good, *g*.)

## LOIRE

### RED

Bourgueil (*e*)
Chinon (*e*)
Coteaux du Loir (*g*)
Coteaux de Saumur (*g*)
Ménetou-Salon (*g*)
St. Nicholas-de-Bourgueil (*v*)
Saumur (*g*)
Saumur-Champigny (*g*)
Touraine (*g*)
Touraine-Amboise (*g*)
Touraine Azay-le-Rideau (*g*)
Touraine-Mesland (*g*)

### WHITE

Anjou (*g*)
Anjou-Coteaux de Loire (*g*)
Anjou Mousseux (*g*)
Anjou-Saumur (*g*)
Blanc Fumé de Pouilly sur Loire (*v*)
Bonnezeaux (*e*)
Chinon (*g*)
Coteaux de l'Aubance (*v*)
Coteaux du Layon (*v*)
Coteaux de Loir (*g*)
Coteaux de Saumur (*g*)
La Coulée de Serrant (*e*)
Jasnières (*v*)
Ménetou-Salon (*v*)
Montlouis (*v*)
Montlouis Mousseux (*v*)
Montlouis Pétillant (*v*)
Muscadet (*g*)
Muscadet de Sèvre-et-Maine (*v*)
Muscadet des Coteaux de la Loire (*v*)
Pouilly-Fumé (*v*)
Pouilly-sur-Loire (*v*)
Quarts de Chaume (*e*)
La Roche aux Moines (*e*)
Quincy (*v*)
Sancerre (*v*)
Saumur (*g*)
Saumur-Mousseux (*g*)
Savennières (*e*)
Touraine (*g*)
Vouvray (*e*)
Vouvray Mousseux (*e*)
Vouvray Pétillant (*e*)

### ROSE

Anjou Rosé de Cabernet (*v*)
Anjou-Saumur (*g*)
Chinon (*g*)
Coteaux de Loir (*g*)
Coteaux de l'Aubance-Rosé de Cabernet (*v*)
Coteaux de la Loire-Rosé de Cabernet (*v*)
Coteaux du Layon-Rosé de Cabernet (*v*)
Coteaux de Saumur-Rosé de Cabernet (*v*)
Coteaux de Saumur (*g*)
Ménetou-Salon (*g*)
Rosé d'Anjou (*v*)
Sancerre (*g*)
Saumur Rosé de Cabernet (*g*)
Touraine (*g*)

## ALSACE

Alsace has hardly done well by the fortunes of war. As its destiny has fluctuated with the movements of politics, so has its wine industry ebbed and flowed in the capricious waters of reputation. But times have changed. Once the world had been reassured that Alsace was still a part of France, its vintners began to rebuild their image as wine people of considerable standing. Old vines were uprooted, and in their place came vineyards of substantial quality. Consumer confidence was further established by building the entire industry around the grape variety itself, with a strict (and unique) insistence on local bottling. Despite a still unduly limited status in the French export trade, the results are decidedly impressive.

Today's Alsatians are known by their varietals, and judged by the name of their shippers—Riesling, Sylvaner, and Gewürztraminer are the primary grapes, while the shipping houses of Dopff, Hugel, and Trimbach have emerged well on the international market. Although there a few instances where the name of the property is actually mentioned (Clos St. Landelin and Clos Ste. Odile, for example), the practice is far from usual. In all cases, the wines of Alsace are characteristically very dry, and, of course, white.

Alsatian Rieslings tend not only to be drier, but also higher in alcohol than their German counterparts, while retaining that pronounced, flowery Riesling nose, with a sound balance of acid and fruit. The Sylvaner, meanwhile, produces a soft, inexpensive white that is almost as versatile as the Riesling in suitably complementing a broad range of simple white meat and fish dishes.

The Alsatian Gewürztraminer is a strikingly unique flavor, extending even to the late-picked levels of borrowed German *Prädikats*. In German, *Gewürz* implies spiciness, and the wines are hardly a disappointment (mostly suited to the more assertive, highly-seasoned hors d'oeuvres and appetizers).

Both the Muscat, which is a sweet wine grape in most parts of the world, and the Tokay d'Alsace are frequently responsible for some charming dry whites, still very much in the Alsatian tradition.

## CHAMPAGNE

It is worth reiterating that Champagne is the name of an area, a specific region close to Paris where a unique and expensive process for the vinification of sparkling wines originated. The principles of the *méthode champenoise,* consisting essentially of an induced secondary (sugar-alcohol) fermentation in the bottle, are discussed at length in Chapter Two.

Although the vineyards of Champagne are rated in a very precise fashion, such classifications are of little relevance to the consumer. Instead, the various Champagne shippers (or "houses" as they are called) blend the wines of several growers to produce a traditional house style—it is precisely this house tradition and the name with which it is associated that become our primary means of identification. Additionally, Champagne is labeled in accordance with its sweetness, beginning with *Brut* (totally dry), and progressing through *Extra Dry*, *Sec*, and *Demi-Sec*, to the very real sweetness of a *Doux*.

The majority of houses are located in two towns, Reims and Épernay. Their products tend to be widely distributed and well-known. In every good wine store several of the following are normally represented:

| | | |
|---|---|---|
| Abel Lepitre | Henriot | Moët & Chandon |
| Ayala | Irroy | Perrier-Jouët |
| Besserat de Bellefan | Jacquesson | Piper-Heidsick |
| Bollinger | Krug | Pol Roger |
| de Castellane | Lanson | Pommery & Greno |
| Charbaut & Fils | Louis Roederer | Ruinart Père & Fils |
| Charles Heidsick | Masse | Taittinger |
| Delbeck | Mercier | de Venoge |
| G.H. Mumm | | Veuve-Clicquot |
| Heidsick Monopole | | Ponsardin |

Champagne is mostly the product of two grapes: the dark-skinned Pinot Noir and the lighter Chardonnay. Although Champagne proper will invariably start out as a still white wine, there remains in some corners of the market a dubious beverage known as Pink Champagne, which derives its color from a brief vatting on the skins of the Pinot Noir. The majority of Champagnes, however, are a blend of white wines from both grapes, the Pinot Noir imparting an obvious sturdiness to the product, in direct proportion to its content. Those made exclusively from Chardonnay are always labeled as *Blanc de Blancs*.

It is only when the production of a certain year is exceptional that the house considers declaring a vintage, which means that throughout the vinification process the wine will be kept separate from that of previous years. So a vintage on a Champagne label really becomes a self-confessed statement of greatness—and, of course, pride. Although all vintage Champagne is, by definition, good, there are inevitably some years that are better than others (notably, 1976, 1975, 1971, 1970, 1969, and 1966). It is the practice of certain firms to produce a special blend made from the very finest of grapes, the formula of which is carefully guarded. These superlative wines are exemplified in Moët et Chandon's Dom Pérignon and its close rival, Comtes de Chartogne *Blanc de Blancs* from Taittinger.

The bulk of Champagne, however, is non-vintage wine—i.e., made from the careful mixing of barrels from different years. To produce an optimum blend is an inescapably long and expensive process, only compounded by the laborious nature of its vinification. The shipper is concerned throughout with the subtle matching of his vast inventory to produce a wine that is consistently representative of years of house tradition. Cheap Champagne is a misnomer.

## THE COUNTRY WINES

The so-called "Country Wines" are those that originate in the minor viticultural regions of France. Confined mostly to the South, they are characteristically straightforward, highly alcoholic beverages, produced in abundance to satisfy the simplest of local needs. While they can on occasion be quite delightful, they are rarely made to last more than a couple of years and require considerable consumer caution in the event that they do show up on the American market. The bulk of the better Country Wines are *Vins Délimités de Qualité Supérieure (V.D.Q.S.)*, a rating that provides a fair assurance of the sound provincial qualities of the wine. Although there are some *Appellations Contrôlées*, only a few are exported with any regularity—notably the whites and rosés of Bandol in Provence, along with the reasonably-priced, almost Rhône-like reds of Côtes du Ventoux, Côtes du Lubéron, and Coteaux du Tricastin.

East of Bordeaux, on the River Lot, we find the famous "black" wines of Cahors (actually only a medium red, similar to the color of a Burgundy). Their best-known representatives are the vineyards of Clos de Gamot and Clos de la Coutale.

Although most of the wines of the Languedoc and Roussillon (including Minervois, Corbières, and Fitou) are only distinguished by their alcohol content, some pleasant fortified beverages are made from the Muscat at Frontignan and Lunel—not unlike the Beaumes de Venise from the southern Rhône.

Much further north (to the east of Burgundy, not far from the Swiss border), the region of the Jura offers a small production of reds, whites, and rosés. More important, however, are the yellow wines (or *vins jaunes*) from Arbois and Château Chalon. Made from the Savagnin grape, *vins jaunes* take advantage of a natural tendency of the area to produce a yeasty film on the surface of aging wines, remarkably like the Spanish *flor*. Unlike fino Sherry, however, the wines are not fortified, but nonetheless retain those same, almost nutty qualities of flavor that can be quite delightful.

In Savoie, further to the south, the crisp whites of Crépy, Apremont, and Seyssel are often too fragile to ship, while the bottle-fermented *(méthode champenoise)* Seyssel sparkling wines have emerged well as substantial, less costly alternatives to Champagne.

Again, we must always remember that, whatever their origins, the Country Wines of France are produced primarily for local consumption: as such they can rarely be expected to survive prolonged aging in the bottle, let alone the traumas of a trans-Atlantic crossing.

# SELECT BIBLIOGRAPHY

Ambrosi, Hans. *Wine Atlas and Dictionary: Germany.* Translated by Bill Gavin. Bielefeld: Ceres-Verlag Rudolf-August Oetker, K.G., 1976.
A detailed reference guide to the theoretical aspects of German wine.

Amerine, M.A.; Berg, H.W.; and Cruess, W.V. *The Technology of Wine Making.* 3rd ed. Westport, Connecticut: Avi Publishing Co., Inc., 1972.
A long and impressively thorough work on the scientific and technical aspects of vinification.

Amerine, Maynard A.; and Roessler, Edward B. *Wines: Their Sensory Evaluation.* San Francisco: W.H. Freeman and Co., 1976.
By far the most impressive current study of the sensory appreciation of wine. A scientific, scholarly approach.

Arlott, John; and Fielden, Christopher. *Burgundy: Vines and Wines.* London: Davies-Poynter Ltd., 1976.
Up-to-date and definitive.

Grossman, Harold J. *Grossman's Guide to Wines, Spirits, and Beers.* 5th ed. New York: Charles Scribner's Sons, 1974.
A good, all-purpose source book, generally aimed at the retailer.

Hallgarten, S.F. *German Wines.* London: Faber and Faber Ltd., 1976.
A mine of detailed information.

Hogg, Anthony. *Guide to Visiting Vineyards.* London: Michael Joseph Ltd., 1976.
An interesting, touring approach with some useful practical information.

Jeffs, Julian. *The Wines of Europe.* London: Faber and Faber Ltd., 1971.
Learned and beautifully written.

Jobé, Joseph, ed. *The Great Book of Wine.* New York: Galahad Books, 1970.
Cleanly arranged, especially its maps and tables.

Johnson, Hugh. *The World Atlas of Wine.* New York: Simon and Schuster, 1971.
Especially useful for its superb, detailed maps.

Lichine, Alexis. *Encyclopedia of Wines and Spirits.* New York: Alfred A. Knopf, Inc., 1967.
A truly monumental work that has become entirely indispensable to the serious enthusiast.

Loeb, O.W.; and Prittie, Terence. *Moselle.* London: Faber and Faber Ltd., 1972.
A thorough, knowledgable study.

Penning-Rowsell, Edmund. *The Wines of Bordeaux.* New York: Stein and Day, 1969.
The authoritative product of years of exhaustive reasearch and experience.

Postgate, Raymond. *The Plain Man's Guide to Wine.* Revised by John Arlott, 1976. London: Michael Joseph Ltd., 1951.
A classic, simple guide with a delightful sense of humor.

Puisais, Jacques; and Chabanon, R.L. *Initiation into the Art of Wine Tasting.* Translated by J.A. Vaccaro. Madison, Wisconsin: Interpublish Inc., 1974.
A valuable handbook on the theory and practice of tasting.

Sichel, Allan. *The Penquin Book of Wines.* Revised by Peter A. Sichel, 2nd ed., 1971. Harmondsworth, England: Penguin Books Ltd., 1965.
A substantial introductory guide.

Vandyke Price, Pamela. *The Taste of Wine.* New York: Random House, Inc., 1975.
Beautifully illustrated with a useful section on food and wine.

Waugh, Alec. *Wines and Spirits.* New York: Time-Life Books, Inc., 1968.
An attractive introduction that communicates the author's deep appreciation for his subject.

Webb, A. Dinsmoor, ed. *Chemistry of Winemaking.* Washington, D.C.: American Chemical Society (Symposium), 1974.
A collection of excellent papers on current advances in the chemistry of wine.

# INDEX

202